Xen Virtualization

A fast and practical guide to supporting multiple operating systems with the Xen hypervisor

Prabhakar Chaganti

BIRMINGHAM - MUMBAI

Xen Virtualization

First published: December 2007

Production Reference: 1181207

Published by Packt Publishing Ltd.
32 Lincoln Road
Olton
Birmingham, B27 6PA, UK.

ISBN 978-1-847192-48-6

www.packtpub.com

Cover image by Bruno Abarca (bruno.granada@gmail.com)

Credits

Author
Prabhakar Chaganti

Reviewer
Paul Wouters
Stefano Maccaglia

Senior Acquisition Editor
David Barnes

Development Editor
Nikhil Bangera

Technical Editor
Akshara Aware

Editorial Team Leader
Mithil Kulkarni

Project Manager
Abhijeet Deobhakta

Project Coordinator
Patricia Weir
Sagara Naik

Indexer
Hemangini Bari

Proofreader
Susan Tase

Production Coordinator
Shantanu Zagade

Cover Designer
Shantanu Zagade

About the Author

Prabhakar Chaganti is the CTO of HelixBrain—a unique startup that provides technology service consulting and is also an incubator that nurtures some very cool software as services applications that are being built on the Ruby on Rails platform.

I would like to thank the reviewer for his helpful and incisive comments, which have helped in making this a better book. The staff at Packt provided great support as always.

This book is dedicated in the memory of my parents—Karunakar and Adilakshmi Chaganti. Lots of love to my wife Nitika whose support and exhortations were the rails upon which this book rolled into the station. Love to my two precious daughters—Anika and Anya.

About the Reviewers

Paul Wouters has been involved with Linux networking and security since he co-founded the Dutch ISP 'Xtended Internet' back in 1996, where he started working with FreeS/WAN IPsec in 1999 and with DNSSEC for the .nl domain in 2001.

He has been writing since 1997, when his first article about network security was published in Linux Journal in 1997. He still writes on occastion for the Dutch "c't Magazine", focussing on Linux, networking and the impact of the digital world on society. He has presented papers at Sans, SecTor, BlackHat, DefCon, CCC, and several other conferences.

He co-founded Xelerance in 2003, focusing on IPsec, DNSSEC, and virtualization, where he is responible for the development of enterprise appliances simplifying the management of these complex security technologies. He is also the release manager for the Linux Openswan IPsec suite.

Stefano Maccaglia is an Italian, Ethical Hacker and Network professional. In 1997, he started his career as a technician in Compaq (Italy). He has worked in Australia, New Zealand, and US and for the past 10 years he has been involved in many projects. Currently, he is a Consultant and Trainer in Poste Italiane, however, he continuously supports the BlackSun Factory Tiger team. Stefano is preparing a book on Network Admission Control framework, which is based on the experience he has gained in the last two years. He participates actively on the security research field.

I would like to thank my wife Lorena for her love, support, and patience. I would also like to thank my entire crew at BlackSun Factory for their friendship, help, and the spirit that they put in the hacking matter and in everyday life.

Table of Contents

Preface

This book covers Xen—an open-source paravirtualization technology that provides a platform for running multiple operating systems on one physical hardware resource, while providing close to native performance. Xen supports several operating systems—Linux, FreeBSD, Windows, and NetBSD. It was originally developed in 2003 at the University of Cambridge Computer Laboratory and now both commercial and free versions of the Xen hypervisor are available. The commercial versions are built on top of the open-source version and have additional enterprise features. In this book we explore and use the open-source version of Xen.

Each chapter in this book is a collection of practical tasks that demonstrates how to achieve common virtualization tasks—you then learn how it works so that you can apply this knowledge to your Xen installation and environment.

What This Book Covers

Chapter 1 introduces the world of Xen and virtualization. It discusses the concepts and advantages of using Xen.

Chapter 2 walks us through the installation of Xen on a Fedora Core system. It discusses installation using yum and also installation by compiling from source.

Chapter 3 creates virtual machines or Xen guest domains that run on top of our Fedora Core system. Ubuntu Feisty, NetBSD, CentOS, and Slackware domains are created.

Chapter 4 explores the management tools available for administering Xen instances. It shows how to install and use xm, XenMan, and virt-manager.

Chapter 5 examines some of the networking options that are available when using Xen and walks through both bridged and routed networking configurations for connecting guest domains to each other as well as to the outside world.

Chapter 6 walks us through some of the storage options that can be used for storing Xen domains. Storage systems such as the file system, Network File System (NFS), and Logical Volume Management (LVM) are discussed.

Chapter 7 shows how to secure Xen domains by encrypting the root file systems. The two techniques covered are plain device mapper-based encryption and key-based encryption using LUKS.

Chapter 8 introduces the options available for the migration of Xen instances. We will save and restore domains, and explore live migration. We will also look at what happens behind the scenes when Xen performs a live migration of a domain.

Chapter 9 talks about some of the newer ideas based on Xen such as libvirt—a virtualization API for interacting with multiple virtualization implementations, and VMCasting—an RSS based technology that can automate the deployment of Xen images using the RSS 2.0 format.

Conventions

In this book, you will find a number of styles of text that distinguish between different kinds of information. Here are some examples of these styles, and an explanation of their meaning.

There are three styles for code. Code words in text are shown as follows: "Create a directory named `xen-images`. We will create all our guest images in this directory."

A block of code will be set as follows:

```
<?xml version="1.0" ?>
<appliance>
  <name xml:lang="en">
```

Any command-line input and output is written as follows:

```
~ make linux-2.6-xenU-config
```

New terms and **important words** are introduced in a bold-type font. Words that you see on the screen, in menus or dialog boxes for example, appear in our text like this: "clicking the **Next** button moves you to the next screen".

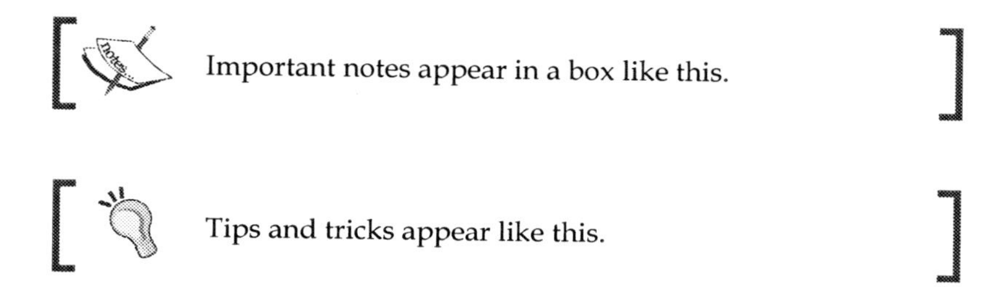

Important notes appear in a box like this.

Tips and tricks appear like this.

Reader Feedback

Feedback from our readers is always welcome. Let us know what you think about this book, what you liked or may have disliked. Reader feedback is important for us to develop titles that you really get the most out of.

To send us general feedback, simply drop an email to `feedback@packtpub.com`, making sure to mention the book title in the subject of your message.

If there is a book that you need and would like to see us publish, please send us a note in the **SUGGEST A TITLE** form on `www.packtpub.com` or email `suggest@packtpub.com`.

If there is a topic that you have expertise in and you are interested in either writing or contributing to a book, see our author guide on `www.packtpub.com/authors`.

Customer Support

Now that you are the proud owner of a Packt book, we have a number of things to help you to get the most from your purchase.

Errata

Although we have taken every care to ensure the accuracy of our contents, mistakes do happen. If you find a mistake in one of our books—maybe a mistake in text or code—we would be grateful if you would report this to us. By doing this you can save other readers from frustration, and help to improve subsequent versions of this book. If you find any errata, report them by visiting `http://www.packtpub.com/support`, selecting your book, clicking on the **Submit Errata** link, and entering the details of your errata. Once your errata are verified, your submission will be accepted and the errata added to the list of existing errata. The existing errata can be viewed by selecting your title from `http://www.packtpub.com/support`.

Questions

You can contact us at `questions@packtpub.com` if you are having a problem with some aspect of the book, and we will do our best to address it.

1 Introduction

Virtualization is a technique of partitioning or dividing the resources of a single server into multiple segregated execution environments. Each of these environments runs independently of the other, thus allowing multiple operating systems to run on the same hardware. This concept has been widely used in the world of mainframe computers over the years, and is now gaining a lot of traction in the world of enterprise IT systems. Each execution environment is called a *guest* and the server on which they execute is called the *host*. The software running on the host that acts as a bridge between the host and the guests, and that enables these multiple execution environments is commonly referred to as the *Virtual Machine Monitor* (VMM) or a *Hypervisor*.

There are three main methodologies used for providing virtualization:

- **System emulation**: The execution environment is called a *virtual machine* and it emulates all the hardware resources. This emulation layer in turn uses the real hardware resources from the host. This enables the emulator to run a guest operating system without any modifications, as the guest OS can use the hardware resources by going through the hardware emulation layer, instead of the real hardware. The VMM executes the CPU instructions that need more privileges than are available in the user space. This approach is followed by products such as VMware (`http://vmware.com/`), Microsoft Virtual PC (`http://www.microsoft.com/windows/products/winfamily/virtualpc/default.mspx`), and Parallels (`http://www.parallels.com/`).

- **Paravirtualization**: There is no hardware emulation. The operating system that runs on a guest needs to be a modified version that is aware of the fact that it is running inside a hypervisor. This cuts down the number of privileged CPU instructions that need to be executed, and as there is no hardware emulation involved, the performance is much better and closer to native speeds. This is the technique used by Xen (`http://www.cl.cam.ac.uk/research/srg/netos/xen/`) and User-Mode Linux (`http://user-mode-linux.sourceforge.net/`).
- **Operating System level virtualization**: Each guest instance is isolated and runs in a secure environment. However, you can execute only multiple instances of guests that run the same operating system as the host. If the host operating system is FreeBSD, you can run only multiple instances of FreeBSD. This is the approach used by the FreeBSD jails (`http://www.freebsd.org/`) and Solaris10 zones (`http://www.sun.com/software/solaris/`).

Hardware emulation introduces some overhead due to the translation of the requests between the hardware and software. The paravirtualized solutions manage to get a speed boost by eliminating the emulation steps. The operating system level virtualization probably has the least overhead among the above three approaches and is the fastest solution. However, it has a limitation that you can only run the same operating system as the host. This takes away one of the great benefits of virtualization, which is to provide users with the ability to run disparate operating systems.

What is Xen?

Xen is an open-source paravirtualization technology that provides a platform for running multiple operating systems in parallel on one physical hardware resource, while providing close to native performance. Xen supports several operating systems—Linux, FreeBSD and NetBSD. The current version of Xen also supports the new generation of AMD Pacifica and Intel VT-x chipsets and can run an OS on these chips without any modifications by using a version of the hypervisor called the *Hardware Virtual Machine* (HVM). HVM mediates between the guest operating system and the hardware and passes on the calls made by the guest to the physical hardware. So you can run Microsoft Windows on these chips using Xen!

Xen was originally developed in 2003 at the University of Cambridge Computer Laboratory (`http://www.cl.cam.ac.uk/research/srg/netos/xen/`). There are both commercial and free versions of Xen. The commercial versions are built on top of the open-source version with additional enterprise features, and are developed and supported by Xensource (`http://www.xensource.com`). The open-source version is developed and maintained by the Xen community. Xen is provided as a part of most of the major Linux distributions including Red Hat Fedora (`http://www.redhat.com`) and SuSe Enterprise Linux (`http://www.novell.com/linux/`). In this book we are going to explore and use the open-source version of Xen.

Some of the highlights of the latest version of Xen are as follows:

- Support for the x86, x86_64, and ia64 architectures.
- Near-native performance in the Xen guests for both CPU and IO-intensive applications.
- Strong isolation between the guests. Isolation provides complete partitioning between the guests whereby each guest runs in its own world and is not affected by any other guest.
- Ability to save and restore domains.
- Live migration from one piece of hardware to another with zero down time.
- HVM support to run unmodified OS on Intel VT-x and AMD Pacifica hardware.
- Scalable to a large number of guests.
- Support for up to 32-way SMP processors.
- A very active open-source community leading the development.
- Support from most major vendors such as IBM, Red Hat, and Novell.

How Does it Work?

Xen refers to each virtual machine that runs on a system as a *domain*. When a Xen server boots up, it first starts the hypervisor, which is responsible for starting a domain named Domain0 (dom0) in which the host operating system runs. dom0 is a privileged domain that can access the hardware resources on the server and also contains tools for managing all the other domains. We will learn how to run Xen in the next chapter. The hypervisor also checks the page tables and is responsible for the allocation of resources for new domains. Each domain interacts with the hypervisor by giving it a hypercall, which is a software trap from the domain to the hypervisor. The hypervisor responds to the hypercall by sending an event to the domain.

New instances of unprivileged domains or virtual machines are created by using the tools that are available in dom0. These tools in turn make calls to the control interface API in the hypervisor to perform the requested operations. These unprivileged domains are referred to as *domU*.

For instance, if you are running a Xen server with three guests, you will have dom0, dom1, and dom2 as the domains on that server. The dom0 is identical to the other domU's, except that it has all the hardware access. We will learn how to create and use new domU instances in Chapter 3.

All requests from the domU instances for hardware access are made to the back-end device drivers in dom0 that will pass on these requests to the actual hardware. This is possible because the guest operating systems are all "aware" that they are running in the Xen hypervisor. The architecture of a Xen system with two guest domains is as follows:

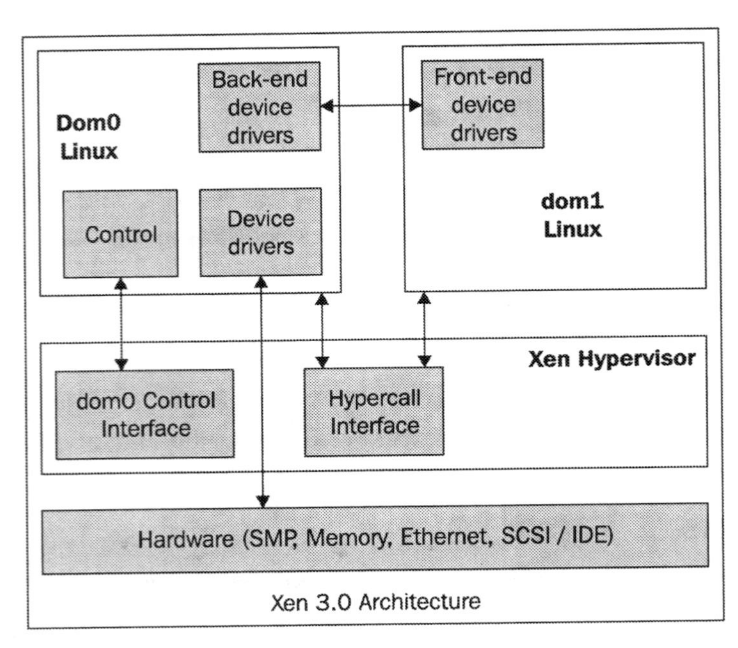

Xen 3.0 Architecture

What Can I Do with It?

Here are some of the cool things that you can do with Xen:

- **Decrease hardware cost**: Reduce the physical space and power requirements by utilizing Xen to decrease the number of maintained physical servers.
- **Improve security**: Protect applications and operating systems by isolating them into virtual machines. We will discuss security in Chapter 7.
- **Increase server utilization**: Consolidate servers to simplify the server management and improve server utilization. This will enable you to use more modular and scalable deployments and centralize the server management. We will learn about the tools for managing domains in Chapter 4.
- **Maintain SLA**: Utilize the live relocation of Xen domains to avoid downtime and maintain your service level agreements. We will explore the migration and backup capabilities of Xen in Chapter 8.
- **Lower TCO**: Adopt the open-source Xen with its tremendous performance benefits and low cost to lower the TCO for your data center or enterprise systems.
- **Improve QA**: Easily test your applications on multiple operating systems without setting up multiple hardware environments.
- **Provision systems**: Provision applications and systems dynamically, quickly, and just in time, by moving virtual machines from one server to another as needed, instead of spending time setting up a new physical server environments. We will learn about relocation of domains in Chapter 8.
- **Clone**: Easily add servers by cloning an existing virtual server.
- **Extend Xen**: Xen is open source. You can extend it to do anything that you need for your specific requirements.
- **Use as Teaching Aid**: Use Xen to set up sandbox environments for students to learn and interact with operating systems, applications or device drivers.
- **Create Virtual applications**: Create domains that encapsulate a specific application, such as a web server or a load balancer. You can then reuse these across the enterprise as needed.
- **Cluster Servers**: Cluster servers to unify multiple servers into a single system.

Xen Terminologies

Following are the definitions for some of the terms used when dealing with Xen technology:

- **VM**: A virtual machine is the virtualized environment that runs an operating system so that the user can run their applications on the operating system.
- **VMM**: The software that provides the ability to run virtual machines.
- **Domain**: The term used by Xen to refer to a virtual machine instance.
- **dom0**: The primary domain in a Xen system. This is the operating system that runs Xen itself.
- **domU**: All the other domains in a Xen system.
- **Host**: The system that provides the environment for running virtual machines.
- **Guest**: The virtual machine instance that runs on a host system.
- **PVM**: Paravirtualized Virtual machine where the Xen domains can only run modified operating systems.
- **HVM**: Full virtualization where the Xen domains can run unmodified operating systems. Xen provides the ability to run Microsoft Windows utilizing this feature.

Summary

This chapter provided an introduction to virtualization and the world of Xen. We also looked at the architecture of Xen and some of the cool things you can do with it. In the next chapter, we will learn how to install and run Xen.

2

Running Xen

In this chapter we will take our first step towards using Xen—installing and then running it. In this chapter we will use Fedora Core 6 as the host operating system; we have chosen Fedora Core 6 as it has good support for Xen. We will first add Xen support to it so that it can be a Xen Domain0 system. In the next chapter we will create guest domains on Fedora Core 6 that run different operating systems. We will assume you have a stock Fedora Core 6 installed and that you are ready to convert it to a Xen. Please make sure you can boot into it without any problems or errors. You can either run Xwindow or work from the console. If you have not installed Fedora Core before and need help with its configuration, the following links could be useful:

- Mauriat's Personal Fedora Core 6 Installation Guide (`http://www.mjmwired.net/resources/mjm-fedora-fc6.html`)
- Softpedia's Install Guide (`http://news.softpedia.com/news/Fedora-Core-6-Installation-Guide-38689.shtml`)
- Howto Forge Guide (http://www.howtoforge.com/installing_a_lamp_system_with_fedora_core_6)

We will explore two different ways of getting Xen installed and running:

- Installing Xen from binary packages
- Installing Xen from the source

Installing Xen from Binary Packages

All the major Linux distributions such as Red Hat, Debian, Ubuntu, SuSe, and Gentoo ship some form of support for using Xen virtualization. In most cases they provide easy to install binary packages in the packaging format used by the specific distributions. This is the easiest and quickest way to get up and running with Xen. In this book we will use Fedora Core 6 from Red Hat as our base operating system and will run other operating systems in virtual machines inside it. The package manager used by Fedora is named *yum*. If you are new to yum and have not used it before, please refer to the Fedora yum manual at `http://fedora.redhat.com/docs/yum/en/`. We will use `yum` to install Xen from the pre-built packages provided by Red Hat. It will install the Xen kernel used by Domain0, the libraries, Python modules, and user space tools used for interacting with Xen.

Time for Action—Installing Xen with yum

yum makes installing Xen in your Fedora Core 6 system a breeze. The following steps are needed to get Xen running:

1. Install the Xen kernel and tools by running the following command:

   ```
   yum install kernel-xen xen
   ```

   This will download and install the following packages and their dependencies:

   - **kernel-xen**: Contains the Xen enabled kernel for both the host and guest operating systems as well as the hypervisor.
   - **xen**: Contains the user-space tools for interacting with the hypervisor.
   - **bridge-utils**: Utilities for configuring the Ethernet bridge that is used for connecting multiple Ethernet devices together.
   - **libvirt**: A C library that provides an API to use the Xen framework.
   - **libvirt-python**: Contains a Python module that let's Python applications to use the API to the Xen framework provided by libvirt.
   - **python-virtinst**: Contains a Python module that uses libvirt for starting installations of Fedora/Red Hat Enterprise Linux related distributions inside virtual machines.
   - **xen-libs**: Contains the libraries needed to run applications to manage Xen.

   Fedora Core 6 uses grub as the bootloader. Installation of the Xen packages from the previous step will add an entry to the `/boot/grub/grub.conf` file for booting the Xen kernel. This is what the `grub.conf` file looks after the installation.

```
# grub.conf generated by anaconda
#
# Note that you do not have to rerun grub after making changes to this file
# NOTICE:  You have a /boot partition.  This means that
#          all kernel and initrd paths are relative to /boot/, eg.
#          root (hd0,1)
#          kernel /vmlinuz-version ro root=/dev/VolGroup00/LogVol00
#          initrd /initrd-version.img
#boot=/dev/hda
default=1
timeout=5
splashimage=(hd0,1)/grub/splash.xpm.gz
hiddenmenu
title Fedora Core (2.6.19-1.2911.6.5.fc6xen)
        root (hd0,1)
        kernel /xen.gz-2.6.19-1.2911.6.5.fc6
        module /vmlinuz-2.6.19-1.2911.6.5.fc6xen ro root=/dev/VolGroup00/LogVol00 rhgb quiet
        module /initrd-2.6.19-1.2911.6.5.fc6xen.img
title Fedora Core (2.6.19-1.2911.6.5.fc6)
        root (hd0,1)
        kernel /vmlinuz-2.6.19-1.2911.6.5.fc6 ro root=/dev/VolGroup00/LogVol00 rhgb quiet
        initrd /initrd-2.6.19-1.2911.6.5.fc6.img
title Fedora Core (2.6.18-1.2798.fc6)
        root (hd0,1)
        kernel /vmlinuz-2.6.18-1.2798.fc6 ro root=/dev/VolGroup00/LogVol00 rhgb quiet
        initrd /initrd-2.6.18-1.2798.fc6.img
title Other
        rootnoverify (hd0,0)
        chainloader +1
```

2. However, Xen kernel is not set as the default boot option. Modify `/boot/grub/grub.conf` and change the value `default=1` to `default=0`. This will change the default kernel used for booting to the Xen kernel instead of the default Fedora kernel. You will need to be the root or a user with administrative privileges in order to do this.
3. Reboot to start using this kernel.
4. Once the machine is up and running, check the version of the running kernel to ensure that you are running the Xen kernel.

```
[root@gandalf pchaganti]# uname -rm
2.6.19-1.2911.6.5.fc6xen x86_64

[root@gandalf pchaganti]#
```

5. The management of domains is done by xend—the Xen Controller daemon. It can be started and stopped using the `/etc/rc.d/init.d/xend` script and is started up by Fedora Core 6 automatically on boot. Check to make sure that `xend` is running by executing the following command to search the list of processes running on the system:

   `pidof xend`

6. Once `xend` is running, it will start Domain0, which is the privileged domain. Check to see that Domain0 has been created and is up and running by using the `xm` command.

```
[root@gandalf pchaganti]# /usr/sbin/xm list
Name                                      ID Mem(MiB) VCPUs State   Time(s)
Domain-0                                   0      931     1 r-----    880.0

[root@gandalf pchaganti]#
```

7. Check to see that all the network interfaces are up. This will include the normal network interfaces such as `eth0` and `lo`, and the Xen related interfaces. The name of the network interface `peth0` that we can see in the following screenshot has changed to `eth0` in the newer versions of Fedora 7.0 and above.

```
[pchaganti@gandalf ~]$ /sbin/ifconfig
eth0      Link encap:Ethernet  HWaddr 00:0F:B0:42:48:F3
          inet addr:192.168.1.176  Bcast:192.168.1.255  Mask:255.255.255.0
          UP BROADCAST RUNNING MULTICAST  MTU:1500  Metric:1
          RX packets:4382 errors:0 dropped:0 overruns:0 frame:0
          TX packets:3079 errors:0 dropped:0 overruns:0 carrier:0
          collisions:0 txqueuelen:0
          RX bytes:3067795 (2.9 MiB)  TX bytes:1044610 (1020.1 KiB)

lo        Link encap:Local Loopback
          inet addr:127.0.0.1  Mask:255.0.0.0
          UP LOOPBACK RUNNING  MTU:16436  Metric:1
          RX packets:1972 errors:0 dropped:0 overruns:0 frame:0
          TX packets:1972 errors:0 dropped:0 overruns:0 carrier:0
          collisions:0 txqueuelen:0
          RX bytes:3293456 (3.1 MiB)  TX bytes:3293456 (3.1 MiB)

peth0     Link encap:Ethernet  HWaddr FE:FF:FF:FF:FF:FF
          UP BROADCAST RUNNING NOARP  MTU:1500  Metric:1
          RX packets:23743 errors:0 dropped:0 overruns:0 frame:0
          TX packets:3319 errors:0 dropped:0 overruns:0 carrier:0
          collisions:561 txqueuelen:1000
          RX bytes:9718036 (9.2 MiB)  TX bytes:1058830 (1.0 MiB)
          Interrupt:18 Base address:0xc800

vif0.0    Link encap:Ethernet  HWaddr FE:FF:FF:FF:FF:FF
          UP BROADCAST RUNNING NOARP  MTU:1500  Metric:1
          RX packets:3079 errors:0 dropped:0 overruns:0 frame:0
          TX packets:4382 errors:0 dropped:0 overruns:0 carrier:0
          collisions:0 txqueuelen:0
          RX bytes:1044610 (1020.1 KiB)  TX bytes:3067795 (2.9 MiB)

xenbr0    Link encap:Ethernet  HWaddr FE:FF:FF:FF:FF:FF
          UP BROADCAST RUNNING NOARP  MTU:1500  Metric:1
          RX packets:768 errors:0 dropped:0 overruns:0 frame:0
          TX packets:0 errors:0 dropped:0 overruns:0 carrier:0
          collisions:0 txqueuelen:0
          RX bytes:202133 (197.3 KiB)  TX bytes:0 (0.0 b)

[pchaganti@gandalf ~]$
```

8. You are now running Xen!

What Just Happened?

We used yum to install the following:

- Xen hypervisor
- dom0 kernel
- Xen libraries and Python modules
- User space tools for interacting with Xen from dom0

The configuration for grub was modified automatically by the installation to add an entry for booting the Xen hypervisor and the dom0 kernel. Let us examine each line that was added as it will give a good insight into the process of what happens when a Xen system boots up. Here is the section that was added for the Xen kernel in the `/boot/grub/grub.conf` (Line numbers have been added and are not actually present in the file):

```
1. title Fedora Core (2.6.19-1.2911.6.5.fc6xen)
2. root (hd0,1)
3. kernel /xen.gz-2.6.19-1.2911.6.5.fc6
4. module /vmlinuz-2.6.19-1.2911.6.5.fc6xen ro root=/dev/VolGroup00/
   LogVol00 rhgb quiet
5. module /initrd-2.6.19-1.2911.6.5.fc6xen.img
```

Line 1 defines the title for this kernel and is displayed in the grub menu on boot, which allows you to select a kernel.

Line 2 defines the root partition that will be used for booting up.

Line 3 specifies the kernel that is to be used for booting. In Xen this specifies the Xen hypervisor and not the dom0 kernel. When a normal Linux is booted, the kernel option refers to an actual Linux kernel.

Line 4 specifies the kernel that is used for booting up the privileged dom0, the root option specifies the partition that holds the root file system, and a few other options, which are not Xen specific but apply to any Linux kernel.

Line 5 defines the file that contains the initial ram disk image that is first loaded by the kernel on initialization before it switches over to using the root file system. This `initrd` image is only suitable for the host and not for any of the guests.

When the machine boots up, it loads the hypervisor that initializes Xen. At this stage you will see a lot of messages flash by on the screen prepended with the text, `[XEN]`. The Xen hypervisor then boots using the dom0 kernel. The operating system that is used by the dom0 kernel contains an `init` script that starts up the Xen daemon—xend, which creates and loads dom0.

The dom0 contains the Xen libraries that provide the API that can be used by client and userland applications to communicate with the Xen framework. The Python modules wrap this functionality so that it can be used by applications written in Python, which is the scripting language used for scripting Xen. We used one of these tools—`xm`, the Xend Manager – to check whether any Xen domains were running. `xm` is the main interface provided for managing the various Xen guest domains. It can be used to create, pause, and shutdown domains. It can also be used, as we did, to list current domains. We are going to look in detail at all the things you can do with `xm` in Chapter 4. Finally we check to make sure that our network interfaces are up. The topic of Xen networking will be covered in detail in Chapter 5. We successfully installed and got Xen running by using the pre-built binary packages provided by Fedora Core 6.

Installing Xen from Source

In the previous section we installed Xen using binary packages. It was quite simple and quick, and enabled us to get Xen running easily especially because the hard job of matching the hypervisor/host/guest kernel options was done by RedHat. However, this means that you depend on the Xen pre-built packages, keeping up with the changes taking place in Xen, which is a fast moving target with bug fixes and features. You cannot take advantage of a brand new feature or a bug fix that was added recently and which is quite crucial for your use. The binary packages usually track the release versions of Xen, so there is no way for you to try out the development versions or the pre-release versions. Here are some reasons why you should get comfortable building Xen from the source code in the Xen revision control repository hosted by Xensource (`http://xenbits.xensource.com/`):

- You can access the latest bug fixes or new features immediately.
- You can experiment with Xen to learn how it works.
- You can extend and build products on top of Xen.
- You can share the bug fixes or improvements you made with the Xen community.
- You can create customized versions of Xen to use within your enterprise or as a commercial product.

In this section we are going to get the latest source code for the next pre-release version of Xen and build it from scratch. We will then install it on our base Fedora system and use it.

Time for Action—Compile Xen

We are going to retrieve the source code, install all the required dependencies, compile the source and, finally, install it on our Fedora Core 6 system.

1. Create a directory that will be used to store the Xen source files and change to this new directory.

   ```
   mkdir ~/xen-source
   cd ~/xen-source
   ```

2. Xen source is stored in a Mercurial revision control repository. You will need to install the mercurial client that can be used for checking out the source code. Use `yum` to install mercurial.

   ```
   yum install mercurial
   ```

   Now we are going to checkout the latest version of the Xen source files. There are several different versions of Xen in the mercurial repository:

   - **xen-3.0.4-testing.hg**: pre-release of the next 3.0.4 version of Xen
   - **xen-3.0.3-testing.hg**: pre-release of the next 3.0.3 version of Xen
   - **xen-3.0.2-testing.hg**: pre-release of the next 3.0.2 version of Xen
   - **xen-2.0-testing.hg**: pre-release of the next 2.0 version of Xen

   We will be using the 3.0.4 version of Xen in this book. Use the mercurial client (`hg`) to check out the source:

```
[pchaganti@gandalf xen-source]$ hg clone http://xenbits.xensource.com/xen-3.0.4-testing.hg
requesting all changes
adding changesets
adding manifests
adding file changes
added 13140 changesets with 91364 changes to 9471 files
3087 files updated, 0 files merged, 0 files removed, 0 files unresolved

[pchaganti@gandalf xen-source]$
```

3. This will create a directory named `xen-3.0.4-testing.hg` under the `xen-source` directory and populate it with the source. The following screenshot shows a listing of the files and directories in it.

```
[pchaganti@gandalf xen-3.0.4-testing.hg]$ ls -al
total 284
drwxrwxr-x 12 pchaganti pchaganti   4096 Mar 13 11:58 .
drwxrwxr-x  3 pchaganti pchaganti   4096 Mar 13 11:55 ..
-rwxrwxr-x  1 pchaganti pchaganti     17 Mar 13 11:58 .bk-to-hg
drwxrwxr-x  3 pchaganti pchaganti   4096 Mar 13 11:58 buildconfigs
drwxrwxr-x  2 pchaganti pchaganti   4096 Mar 13 11:58 config
-rw-rw-r--  1 pchaganti pchaganti   2185 Mar 13 11:58 Config.mk
-rw-rw-r--  1 pchaganti pchaganti  19355 Mar 13 11:58 COPYING
drwxrwxr-x  7 pchaganti pchaganti   4096 Mar 13 11:58 docs
drwxrwxr-x  3 pchaganti pchaganti   4096 Mar 13 11:58 extras
drwxrwxr-x  3 pchaganti pchaganti   4096 Mar 13 11:58 .hg
-rw-rw-r--  1 pchaganti pchaganti   6059 Mar 13 11:58 .hgignore
-rw-rw-r--  1 pchaganti pchaganti   1178 Mar 13 11:58 .hgtags
-rwxrwxr-x  1 pchaganti pchaganti     17 Mar 13 11:58 .hg-to-bk
-rwxrwxr-x  1 pchaganti pchaganti   1161 Mar 13 11:58 install.sh
drwxrwxr-x 11 pchaganti pchaganti   4096 Mar 13 11:58 linux-2.6-xen-sparse
-rw-rw-r--  1 pchaganti pchaganti   6663 Mar 13 11:58 Makefile
drwxrwxr-x  3 pchaganti pchaganti   4096 Mar 13 11:58 patches
-rw-rw-r--  1 pchaganti pchaganti   7096 Mar 13 11:58 README
-rw-rw-r--  1 pchaganti pchaganti 110128 Mar 13 11:58 .rootkeys
drwxrwxr-x 30 pchaganti pchaganti   4096 Mar 13 11:58 tools
drwxrwxr-x  3 pchaganti pchaganti   4096 Mar 13 11:58 unmodified_drivers
drwxrwxr-x  8 pchaganti pchaganti   4096 Mar 13 11:58 xen

[pchaganti@gandalf xen-3.0.4-testing.hg]$
```

We are ready to compile Xen. We need to install the pre-requisite packages that provide the compiler, libraries, and development headers required for setting up a Xen development environment. Here are the packages that need to be installed on a Fedora Core 6 machine. If you have already compiled C code on your machine, you may have some of these installed.

- **gcc:** Contains the GNU Compiler Collection version 4.0 and is needed for compiling C code.
- **glibc-devel**: Contains the object files necessary for developing programs, which use the standard C libraries.
- **libgomp**: Contains GCC shared support library, which is needed for OpenMP 2.5 support.
- **glibc-headers**: Contains the header files necessary for developing programs, which use the standard C libraries.
- **ncurses-devel**: The header files and libraries for developing applications that use the ncurses terminal handling library.

- **openssl-devel**: Contains static libraries and include files needed to develop applications that support various cryptographic algorithms and protocols.
- **zlib-devel**: Contains the header files and libraries needed to develop programs that use the zlib compression and decompression library.
- **xorg-X11-proto-devel**: Contains all necessary include files and libraries needed to develop X11 applications.
- **python-devel**: Contains the header files and libraries needed to develop Python extensions.
- **tetex-latex**: Contains the LaTeX front end for the TeX text formatting system that is used for producing the documentation for Xen.
- **xen-devel**: Contains the libraries and header files that are needed for compiling Xen from source.

Install these packages using yum:

```
yum install gcc glibc-devel xen-devel libgomp glibc-headers
  ncurses-devel openssl-devel zlib-devel xorg-X11-proto-devel
    python-devel tetex-latex
```

4. The first step before we compile the kernel is to configure it. The following command will bring up the familiar Linux kernel configuration dialog. Accept the defaults unless you need to make changes to add support for some drivers or other options. Exit the dialog and save the changes when asked.

```
make linux-2.6-xen0-config
```

5. Compile the kernel and the modules.

```
make linux-2.6-xen0-build
```

6. The above command will compile and install the various artifacts from the build into the `dist/install` directory.

```
[pchaganti@gandalf xen-3.0.4-testing.hg]$ ls -al dist/install/
total 28
drwxrwxr-x 4 pchaganti pchaganti 4096 Mar 13 13:24 .
drwxrwxr-x 3 pchaganti pchaganti 4096 Mar 13 13:04 ..
drwxrwxr-x 2 pchaganti pchaganti 4096 Mar 13 13:24 boot
drwxrwxr-x 3 pchaganti pchaganti 4096 Mar 13 13:04 lib

[pchaganti@gandalf xen-3.0.4-testing.hg]$
```

The boot directory contains the configuration used for this Xen kernel, the kernel image, and the kernel debugging symbols files.

```
[pchaganti@gandalf xen-3.0.4-testing.hg]$ ls -al dist/install/boot/
total 10048
drwxrwxr-x 2 pchaganti pchaganti    4096 Mar 13 13:24 .
drwxrwxr-x 4 pchaganti pchaganti    4096 Mar 13 13:24 ..
-rw-rw-r-- 1 pchaganti pchaganti   27305 Mar 13 13:24 config-2.6.16.38-xen0
-rw-rw-r-- 1 pchaganti pchaganti 1031043 Mar 13 13:24 System.map-2.6.16.38-xen0
-rw-r--r-- 1 pchaganti pchaganti 9955671 Mar 13 13:24 vmlinux-syms-2.6.16.38-xen0
-rw-r--r-- 1 pchaganti pchaganti 2461962 Mar 13 13:24 vmlinuz-2.6.16.38-xen0
lrwxrwxrwx 1 pchaganti pchaganti      22 Mar 13 13:24 vmlinuz-2.6.16-xen0 -> vmlinuz-2.6.16.38-xen0
lrwxrwxrwx 1 pchaganti pchaganti      22 Mar 13 13:24 vmlinuz-2.6-xen0 -> vmlinuz-2.6.16.38-xen0

[pchaganti@gandalf xen-3.0.4-testing.hg]$
```

The lib directory contains all the kernel modules and drivers.

```
[pchaganti@gandalf xen-3.0.4-testing.hg]$ ls -al dist/install/lib/modules/2.6.16.38-xen0/
total 20
drwxrwxr-x 3 pchaganti pchaganti 4096 Mar 13 13:07 .
drwxrwxr-x 3 pchaganti pchaganti 4096 Mar 13 13:04 ..
lrwxrwxrwx 1 pchaganti pchaganti   68 Mar 13 13:04 build -> /home/pchaganti/xen-source/xen-3.0.4-testin
g.hg/linux-2.6.16.38-xen0
drwxrwxr-x 7 pchaganti pchaganti 4096 Mar 13 13:07 kernel
lrwxrwxrwx 1 pchaganti pchaganti   68 Mar 13 13:07 source -> /home/pchaganti/xen-source/xen-3.0.4-testi
ng.hg/linux-2.6.16.38-xen0

[pchaganti@gandalf xen-3.0.4-testing.hg]$
```

7. Install these artifacts on to your system by running the following command as root. This will install the kernel modules and copy the kernel image and symbol files to `/boot`.

   `make linux-2.6-xen0-install`

Following are the files in the /boot directory after running the above command.

```
[root@gandalf xen-3.0.4-testing.hg]# ls -al /boot
total 27812
drwxr-xr-x  4 root root    1024 Mar 13 13:38 .
drwxr-xr-x 24 root root    4096 Mar 13 12:29 ..
-rw-rw-r--  1 root root   27305 Mar 13 13:38 config-2.6.16.38-xen0
-rw-r--r--  1 root root   63345 Oct 16 14:52 config-2.6.18-1.2798.fc6
-rw-r--r--  1 root root   66774 Mar  4 16:18 config-2.6.19-1.2911.6.5.fc6
-rw-r--r--  1 root root   66150 Mar  4 16:36 config-2.6.19-1.2911.6.5.fc6xen
drwxr-xr-x  2 root root    1024 Mar 13 09:48 grub
-rw-------  1 root root 2362580 Mar 12 00:48 initrd-2.6.18-1.2798.fc6.img
-rw-------  1 root root 2378006 Mar 11 22:05 initrd-2.6.19-1.2911.6.5.fc6.img
-rw-------  1 root root 2356708 Mar 11 22:53 initrd-2.6.19-1.2911.6.5.fc6xen.img
drwx------  2 root root   12288 Mar 11 20:40 lost+found
-rw-r--r--  1 root root   95894 Oct 16 14:53 symvers-2.6.18-1.2798.fc6.gz
-rw-r--r--  1 root root   98772 Mar  4 16:18 symvers-2.6.19-1.2911.6.5.fc6.gz
-rw-r--r--  1 root root   98984 Mar  4 16:37 symvers-2.6.19-1.2911.6.5.fc6xen.gz
-rw-rw-r--  1 root root 1031043 Mar 13 13:38 System.map-2.6.16.38-xen0
-rw-r--r--  1 root root 1123473 Oct 16 14:52 System.map-2.6.18-1.2798.fc6
-rw-r--r--  1 root root 1165375 Mar  4 16:18 System.map-2.6.19-1.2911.6.5.fc6
-rw-r--r--  1 root root 1128560 Mar  4 16:36 System.map-2.6.19-1.2911.6.5.fc6xen
-rw-r--r--  1 root root 9955671 Mar 13 13:38 vmlinux-syms-2.6.16.38-xen0
-rw-r--r--  1 root root 2461962 Mar 13 13:38 vmlinuz-2.6.16.38-xen0
lrwxrwxrwx  1 root root      22 Mar 13 13:38 vmlinuz-2.6.16-xen0 -> vmlinuz-2.6.16.38-xen0
-rw-r--r--  1 root root 1979774 Oct 16 14:52 vmlinuz-2.6.18-1.2798.fc6
-rw-r--r--  1 root root 2144590 Mar  4 16:18 vmlinuz-2.6.19-1.2911.6.5.fc6
-rw-r--r--  1 root root 2058745 Mar  4 16:36 vmlinuz-2.6.19-1.2911.6.5.fc6xen
lrwxrwxrwx  1 root root      22 Mar 13 13:38 vmlinuz-2.6-xen0 -> vmlinuz-2.6.16.38-xen0
-rw-r--r--  1 root root  274655 Mar  4 15:45 xen.gz-2.6.19-1.2911.6.5.fc6
-rwxr-xr-x  1 root root  638376 Mar  4 17:11 xen-syms-2.6.19-1.2911.6.5.fc6

[root@gandalf xen-3.0.4-testing.hg]#
```

8. Run depmod to create a list of module dependencies by reading each module under /lib/modules/2.6.16.38-xen0 and to determine what symbols it exports, and what symbols it needs

    depmod -a 2.6.16.38-xen0

9. Create the `initrd` in the `boot` dir that will be used by the Xen kernel while booting.

```
[root@gandalf xen-3.0.4-testing.hg]# /sbin/mkinitrd -v -f --with=sd_mod --with=scsi_mod /boot/in
itrd-2.6.16.38-xen0.img 2.6.16.38-xen0
Creating initramfs
Looking for deps of module uhci-hcd
Looking for deps of module ohci-hcd
Looking for deps of module ehci-hcd
Looking for deps of module ext3
Looking for driver for device hda3
Looking for deps of module ide:m-disk
Looking for deps of module pci:v000010DEd000000D5sv000010DEsd00000C80bc01sc01i8a
Looking for deps of module sata_nv
Looking for deps of module ide-disk
Looking for deps of module dm-mod
Looking for deps of module dm-mirror
Looking for deps of module dm-zero
Looking for deps of module dm-snapshot
Looking for deps of module sd_mod
Looking for deps of module scsi_mod
Looking for deps of module sd_mod
Using modules:
/sbin/nash -> /tmp/initrd.ds7015/bin/nash
/sbin/insmod.static -> /tmp/initrd.ds7015/bin/insmod
/sbin/lvm.static -> /tmp/initrd.ds7015/bin/lvm
/etc/lvm -> /tmp/initrd.ds7015/etc/lvm
`/etc/lvm/lvm.conf' -> `/tmp/initrd.ds7015/etc/lvm/lvm.conf'

[root@gandalf xen-3.0.4-testing.hg]#
```

Compile and install the various Xen tools, libraries and Python modules. Please make sure that you don't have the Xen tools binary package installed before doing this.

```
make install KERNELS="linux-2.6-xen0"
```

10. Modify grub to add an entry for booting this new Xen kernel.

```
# grub.conf generated by anaconda
#
# Note that you do not have to rerun grub after making changes to this file
# NOTICE:  You have a /boot partition.  This means that
#          all kernel and initrd paths are relative to /boot/, eg.
#          root (hd0,1)
#          kernel /vmlinuz-version ro root=/dev/VolGroup00/LogVol00
#          initrd /initrd-version.img
#boot=/dev/hda
default=0
timeout=5
splashimage=(hd0,1)/grub/splash.xpm.gz
hiddenmenu
title Fedora Core (2.6.16-38-xen0)
        root (hd0,1)
        kernel /xen.gz
        module /vmlinuz-2.6-xen0 ro root=/dev/VolGroup00/LogVol00 rhgb quiet
        module /initrd-2.6.16.38-xen0.img
title Fedora Core (2.6.19-1.2911.6.5.fc6)
        root (hd0,1)
        kernel /vmlinuz-2.6.19-1.2911.6.5.fc6 ro root=/dev/VolGroup00/LogVol00 rhgb quiet
        initrd /initrd-2.6.19-1.2911.6.5.fc6.img
title Fedora Core (2.6.18-1.2798.fc6)
        root (hd0,1)
        kernel /vmlinuz-2.6.18-1.2798.fc6 ro root=/dev/VolGroup00/LogVol00 rhgb quiet
        initrd /initrd-2.6.18-1.2798.fc6.img
title Other
        rootnoverify (hd0,0)
        chainloader +1
~
"/boot/grub/grub.conf" 29L, 1020C
```

11. Reboot into your new Xen system!

12. Check to make sure that everything started up fine.

```
[root@gandalf pchaganti]# /usr/sbin/xm list
Name                                      ID Mem(MiB) VCPUs State   Time(s)
Domain-0                                   0      934     1 r-----    370.6

[root@gandalf pchaganti]#
```

13. Check the network interfaces to make sure they are all up and running.

```
[pchaganti@gandalf ~]$ /sbin/ifconfig
eth0      Link encap:Ethernet  HWaddr 00:0F:B0:42:48:F3
          inet addr:192.168.1.176  Bcast:192.168.1.255  Mask:255.255.255.0
          UP BROADCAST RUNNING MULTICAST  MTU:1500  Metric:1
          RX packets:17428 errors:0 dropped:0 overruns:0 frame:0
          TX packets:10267 errors:0 dropped:0 overruns:0 carrier:0
          collisions:0 txqueuelen:0
          RX bytes:21688288 (20.6 MiB)  TX bytes:897646 (876.6 KiB)

lo        Link encap:Local Loopback
          inet addr:127.0.0.1  Mask:255.0.0.0
          UP LOOPBACK RUNNING  MTU:16436  Metric:1
          RX packets:6433 errors:0 dropped:0 overruns:0 frame:0
          TX packets:6433 errors:0 dropped:0 overruns:0 carrier:0
          collisions:0 txqueuelen:0
          RX bytes:9248052 (8.8 MiB)  TX bytes:9248052 (8.8 MiB)

peth0     Link encap:Ethernet  HWaddr FE:FF:FF:FF:FF:FF
          UP BROADCAST RUNNING NOARP  MTU:1500  Metric:1
          RX packets:19784 errors:0 dropped:0 overruns:0 frame:0
          TX packets:10371 errors:0 dropped:0 overruns:0 carrier:0
          collisions:2346 txqueuelen:1000
          RX bytes:22499297 (21.4 MiB)  TX bytes:904534 (883.3 KiB)
          Interrupt:17 Base address:0x7000

vif0.0    Link encap:Ethernet  HWaddr FE:FF:FF:FF:FF:FF
          UP BROADCAST RUNNING NOARP  MTU:1500  Metric:1
          RX packets:10267 errors:0 dropped:0 overruns:0 frame:0
          TX packets:17428 errors:0 dropped:0 overruns:0 carrier:0
          collisions:0 txqueuelen:0
          RX bytes:897646 (876.6 KiB)  TX bytes:21688288 (20.6 MiB)

xenbr0    Link encap:Ethernet  HWaddr FE:FF:FF:FF:FF:FF
          UP BROADCAST RUNNING NOARP  MTU:1500  Metric:1
          RX packets:65 errors:0 dropped:0 overruns:0 frame:0
          TX packets:0 errors:0 dropped:0 overruns:0 carrier:0
          collisions:0 txqueuelen:0
          RX bytes:17144 (16.7 KiB)  TX bytes:0 (0.0 b)


[pchaganti@gandalf ~]$ █
```

You have successfully compiled and installed the development version of Xen in your machine and are now running it.

What Just Happened?

The source code for Xen is stored in a mercurial repository that is hosted at `http://xenbits.xensource.com`. This is a public repository and contains the source code for the open-source version of Xen. The code is tagged with different versions for the stable and development versions. The stable released versions are usually the ones that are available as pre-built packages. In the previous section we used the pre-built packages for Xen 3.0.4 provided by Fedora Core 6. However, there is a new pre-release version of Xen that has several bug fixes and enhancements. It would be nice to use this or any other version of Xen for that matter, without depending on a pre-built package of Xen. We first installed the mercurial client used for retrieving the source. We also installed all the pre-requisites for compiling C code including the *gcc* compiler collection. You may already have some of these packages if you have ever compiled C code on your system. Also, there are some libraries such as *openssl* and *zlib* that are needed to compile Xen.

The `Makefile` provided with the Xen distribution has several pre-defined targets that we can use for compiling Xen. the following were used in this section:

- **linux-2.6-xen0-config**: This target is used for configuring the dom0 kernel. The default will configure the linux kernel using the familiar **menuconfig** option that brings up a **ncurses** dialog based configuration utility. You can configure the various options to fine tune the dom0 kernel to your specifications. You can also select a different interface for configuration. Running this target for the first time will download linux-2.6.16.38 from `http://kernel.org` to the current directory. This unmodified kernel is referred to as a *pristine kernel*. It is downloaded and stored locally in a directory called `pristine-linux` and is also archived to a `bzip` file. A dom0 directory named `linux-2.6.16.38-xen0` is created, Xen patches are then applied to the pristine kernel in this directory to create the dom0 kernel. This is the kernel that is configured when we run this target. If you are new to Linux kernel configuration the following resources will be useful:
    - **Kernel Rebuild Guide** (`http://www.digitalhermit.com/linux/Kernel-Build-HOWTO.html`)
    - **Nixcraft Guide** (`http://www.cyberciti.biz/tips/print.php?p=710&print=1`)
    - **Linux focus Guide** (`http://linuxfocus.org/English/July2002/article252.shtml`)

- **linux-2.6-xen0-build**: This target compiles the kernel and the modules using the configuration from the previous step. The compiled kernel and modules are installed into a `dist/install` directory created within the current directory.
- **linux-2.6-xen0-install**: This target will take everything from the `dist/install` directory and install it on to the local system. The kernel and the kernel configuration file are copied to the `/boot` directory along with the kernel symbols file that is helpful for debugging. In order to do this you must have administrative privileges. So either use `sudo` or become the super user by using `su` before you execute this target.
- **install KERNELS="linux-2.6-xen0"**: This target will compile the Xen libraries and Python modules and install them on to the system. Once again you will need administrative privileges in order to do this.

We have installed most of the things needed to run the pre-release version of Xen. After the compilation, we also created an `initrd` image that can be used for booting. This was automatically installed for us when we installed Xen using a pre-built package. Since we compiled the kernel ourselves in this section, we created the `initrd` image by using the `mkinitrd` command. Finally we added an entry to the `/boot/grub/grub.conf` to boot our new pre-release version of Xen.

Summary

In this chapter we took our first steps with Xen and learned two different ways to get Xen installed and running on our system:

- We installed Xen using the pre-built binary packages provided by Red Hat for the Fedora Core 6 distribution.
- We checked out the pre-release version of Xen from the Mercury Revision Control Repository, and compiled and installed Xen from scratch.

In the next chapter, we will create virtual machines or domUs that will run different operating systems, inside our base Fedora Core 6 system.

3

Creating Virtual Machines

In this chapter we will create new virtual machines, running different operating systems, which will be hosted by the Xen instance we set up in the previous chapter. Each of these virtual machines is referred to as a guest domain in Xen parlance. Our base system that runs dom0 is Fedora Core 6. By the end of this chapter we will have Fedora Core 6 running four different guest domains under Xen. We will use a different installation method for each domain, so that by the end of this chapter you will be familiar with the most common permutations involved in creating domains using Xen.

We will create the following guest domains:

- Ubuntu Feisty
- NetBSD
- CentOS
- Slackware

A Plan for Creating Xen Domains

We will use the following strategy when creating the guest domains in this chapter:

1. Choose the storage medium for the domain—files, partitions, LVM, etc. We have exclusively used files in this chapter for ease of use.
2. Install files for the guest operating system in the chosen storage medium. The mechanism for installing the files can be a bootstrapping tool such as *debootstrap*, an iso image file, a cd-rom, or even a simple file system directory that contains all the files needed.

3. Create a configuration file that specifies the parameters that will be used by Xen when creating the domain. We will examine all the various configuration options that can be used in the next chapter.
4. Create the domain using `xm`. We will explore the `xm` tool in detail in the next chapter.

The above is a workflow that addresses the various aspects essential for generating a working Xen environment for the guest operating system of your choice. You can also download ready-to-use Xen images from several sites on the Internet. You may or may not get the exact image you are looking for, but it's worth checking these sites out:

- Jailtime: `http://jailtime.org/`
- Oszoo: `http://www.oszoo.org/wiki/index.php/Category:OS_images`

Physical Address Extension

Physical Address Extension (PAE) is a technology that increases the amount of physical or virtual memory available to user mode applications and thus allows servers to access physical memory beyond 4 GB. In order to achieve this, PAE modifies the 32-bit addressing mode to a 64-bit addressing mode, and thus allows the operating system and user applications to access the additional physical memory. This can significantly enhance the performance of the operating system, which is valuable especially when the server is hosting multiple operating systems. Both the Linux kernel and the Xen hypervisor can benefit from of PAE if it is present. The three modes that are available for running Xen are as follows:

- Pure 32-bit mode.
- 32-bit mode with PAE.
- Pure 64-bit mode.

There are some important things to consider when using these modes:

- The Xen hypervisor, dom0, and domU must run in the same mode when using paravirtualization. This means that when using paravirtualization, if the hypervisor is running in 32 bit mode, then the dom0 and all the domU instances must also run in the 32 bit mode, and not in the PAE or 64 bit modes. You cannot currently mix and match different modes of Xen.
- The above restriction does not apply when using full virtualization or Hardware Virtual Machine (HVM). Currently you can only use HVM with supported chipsets from Intel and AMD. Here is the current list of HVM compatible processors:
  `http://wiki.xensource.com/xenwiki/HVM_Compatible_Processors`

The server that runs my Xen system does not have any of the newer chipsets from Intel or AMD. It is a 32-bit machine with 1GB of memory. However, most of the current distributions, including Fedora Core ship a PAE enabled Xen hypervisor, which will not work on servers such as mine. There are two workarounds for this issue—recompile the distribution-specific Xen packages to use a non-PAE kernel or use the current 3.0.4 version source from Xen and build the hypervisor and kernels yourselves. For Fedora, you can recompile using the source RPM after disabling the PAE configuration option in the spec file for the SRPM. I used the second option as it enables the use of the most recent versions of Xen. We have already learnt how to compile the Xen hypervisor and dom0 kernel in the previous chapter. These will be the default non-PAE versions. You can check if you have a PAE enabled kernel installed by running the `cpuinfo` command:

```
~ cat /proc/cpuinfo
```

The machine with an AMD processor shows the following output:

```
processor       : 0
vendor_id       : AuthenticAMD
cpu family      : 15
model           : 47
model name      : AMD Sempron(tm) Processor 3400+
stepping        : 2
cpu MHz         : 1989.897
cache size      : 128 KB
fdiv_bug        : no
hlt_bug         : no
f00f_bug        : no
coma_bug        : no
fpu             : yes
fpu_exception   : yes
cpuid level     : 1
wp              : yes

flags           : fpu tsc msr pae mce cx8 apic mtrr mca cmov pat pse36
                  clflush mmx fxsr sse sse2 syscall nx mmxext fxsr_opt
                  lm 3dnowext 3dnow pni lahf_lm ts fid vid ttp tm stc

bogomips        : 3980.93
```

If the flags section above displays a flag named `pae`, then you have a processor that supports PAE, otherwise your processor does not support PAE and you will need to use a non-PAE kernel.

Compiling a domU Kernel

In this section we are going to compile a domU kernel, an unprivileged kernel and which will be used by the guest domains or virtual machines. We are going to use the Xen 3.0.4 source that we downloaded in the previous chapter and build the domU kernel.

1. Change to the directory that contains the source.

   ```
   ~ cd /home/pchaganti/xen-source/xen-3.0.4-testing.hg
   ```

2. Configure the domU kernel.

   ```
   ~ make linux-2.6-xenU-config
   ```

3. Select the options that you want for your domU kernel. If you are not sure, opt for the default settings. Ensure that PAE is disabled by navigating through the following screens under the **Processor type and features** menu and making sure that the **High Memory Support** is set either to **off** or **4GB**. Save your configuration when you exit.

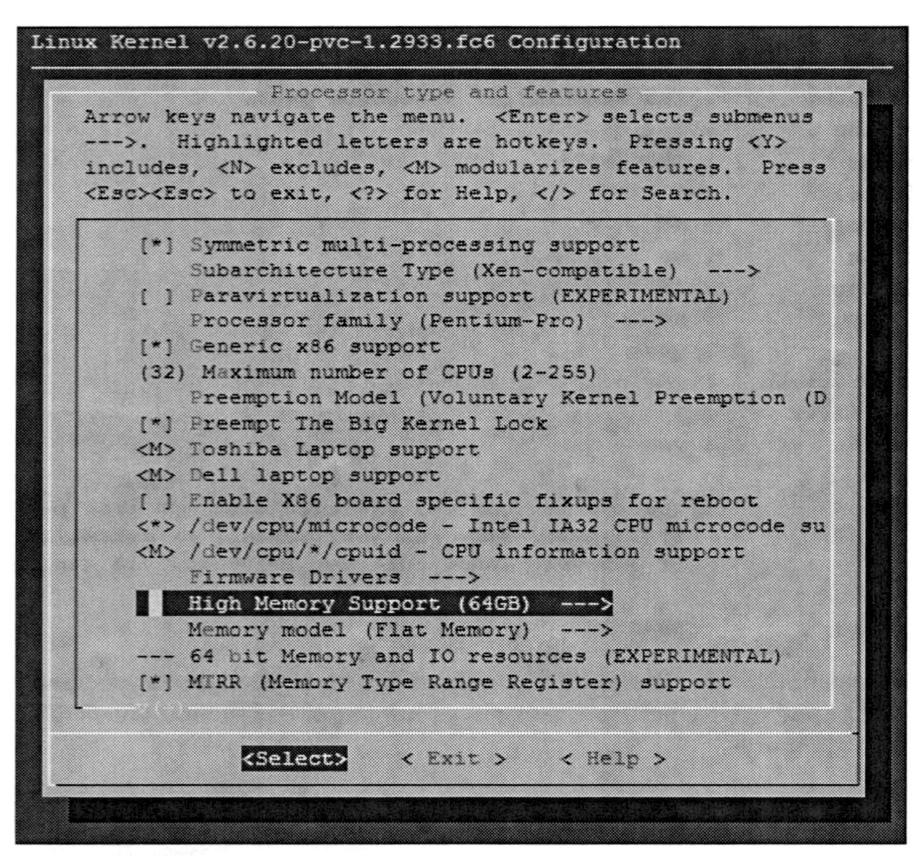

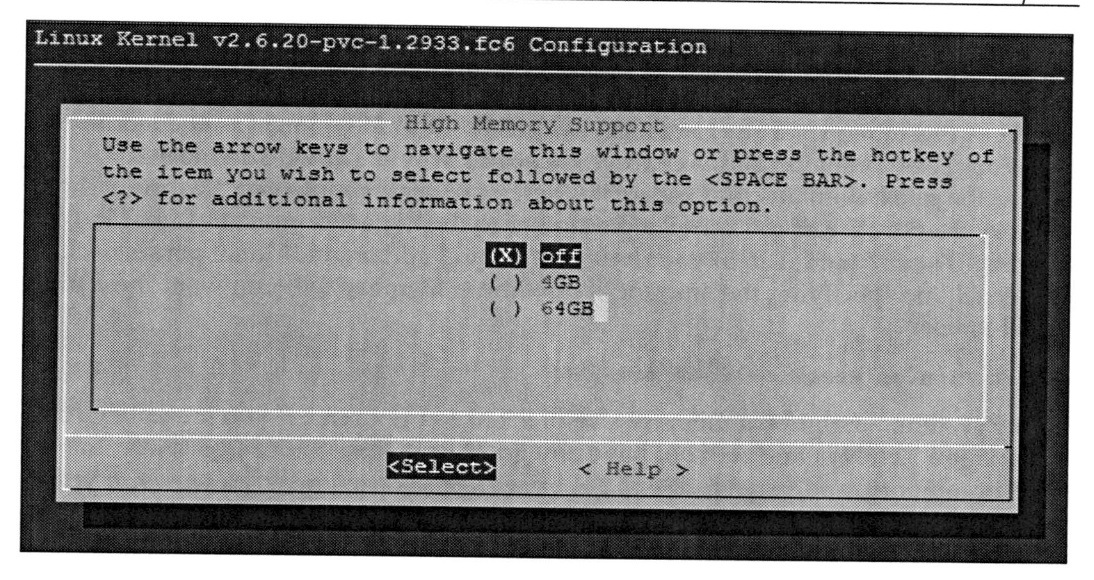

4. Build the domU kernel and then install it.

   ```
   make linux-2.6-xenU-build
   make linux-2.6-xenU-install
   ```

5. Create an initrd for the domU kernel.

   ```
   # mkinitrd -v -f --with=ide-disk --with=sd_mod --with=ide-generic
     --with=ext3 --with=scsi_mod /boot/initrd-2.6.16.38-xenU.img
      2.6.16.38-xenU
   ```

6. Here is what my `/boot` directory looked like with the domU kernel related files after the installation from the previous step was completed.

```
[root@gandalf pchaganti]# ls -l /boot/*xenU*
-rw-rw-r-- 1 root root   19755 Apr  1 23:21 /boot/config-2.6.16.38-xenU
-rw------- 1 root root 2060070 Apr  2 05:10 /boot/initrd-2.6.16.38-xenU.img
-rw-rw-r-- 1 root root  456696 Apr  1 23:21 /boot/System.map-2.6.16.38-xenU
-rw-r--r-- 1 root root 2781812 Apr  1 23:21 /boot/vmlinux-syms-2.6.16.38-xenU
-rw-r--r-- 1 root root 1085386 Apr  1 23:21 /boot/vmlinuz-2.6.16.38-xenU
lrwxrwxrwx 1 root root      22 Apr  1 23:21 /boot/vmlinuz-2.6.16-xenU -> vmlinuz-2.6.16.38-xenU
lrwxrwxrwx 1 root root      22 Apr  1 23:21 /boot/vmlinuz-2.6-xenU -> vmlinuz-2.6.16.38-xenU
[root@gandalf pchaganti]#
```

7. Now we have a domU kernel compiled and ready and we will use it to boot the virtual machines that we will create later in the chapter.

Xen Domain Memory

In our current configuration, the dom0 kernel takes up all the memory available within the system on start up, and then assigns it out to the domUs as needed. When we create guest domains in this chapter we need a way to provide memory for each of the guest domains that we create. Xen provides a simple way to specify the memory used by the dom0 kernel a parameter to the hypervisor on start up. Modify the `/boot/grub/menu.lst` in your base system and add an additional parameter to the kernel line specifying the amount of maximum memory that you want the dom0 kernel to use:

```
kernel /xen.gz noreboot dom0_mem=256M
```

On my system, I assigned a memory size of 256M to my dom0. If you are only going to manage a Xen host and will not have any guest domains, you can go lower than 256M of memory, and may be able to get by with 96M of memory. However, if you are using any guest domains, you will need to ensure that you have enough memory available to be assigned to the guests as they start up. In this case you should set the memory to at least 512M. When we create new guest domains in this chapter, we will specify the maximum memory to be used by each of the guest domains in the configuration file for the domain.

Pygrub

The normal way in Xen is to specify the kernel and initrd from within the config file in dom0. This means that any time the kernel needs to be modified or changed, you will need administrative privileges on dom0 host in order to modify it. Redhat developed a bootloader named pygrub that works in a similar way to grub, and allows domU users to pick their own kernel using the same user interface as grub. Xen starts pygrub before the domUs start. The console user can select the kernel to boot from a menu that reads from the same configuration file as grub— `/grub/menu.lst`. Once the user selects a kernel and initrd, control is returned back to Xen and it starts the selected domU kernel. In this chapter we are using the plain Xen way of specifying the kernel and initrd in the configuration file, but you need to be aware of the pygrub option as it can come in handy in several Xen environments.

Ubuntu Feisty

Ubuntu is a community developed Linux based on *Debian* that has become probably one of the most popular Linux distributions in the world (`http://www.ubuntu.com/`). It has a huge user base that is growing very rapidly and it releases new versions every six months. We are going to use the beta version of Ubuntu Feisty and create a virtual machine or guest domain that runs it.

Time for Action—Bootstrapping an Ubuntu System

1. Ubuntu uses the Debian tool called *debootstrap* for creating a system from scratch. This is not currently available in the Fedora repositories. There are some much older rpms available on the net. We will download the latest version of *debootstrap* from Ubuntu Feisty and install it on our Fedora Core base system. As this is in a deb format, we will convert it into a format suitable for installation on a Fedora system. Get the following two dependencies and install them first.

```
~ wget http://www.hccfl.edu/pollock/AUnix1/alien/deb-1.10.27-
    3.i586.rpm
~ wget http://www.hccfl.edu/pollock/AUnix1/alien/html2text-1.3.2a-
    3.i586.rpm
# rpm -ivh --nodeps deb-1.10.27-3.i586.rpm
# rpm -ivh --nodeps html2text-1.3.2a-3.i586.rpm
```

2. Download and install *alien* for converting packages from one distribution format to the other.

```
~ wget http://www.hccfl.edu/pollock/AUnix1/alien/alien_8.64.tar.gz
~ tar -zxvf alien_8.64.tar.gz
~ perl Makefile.PL
~ make PREFIX=/usr
# make PREFIX=/usr install
```

3. Download *debootstrap* from Ubuntu, convert it to rpm format and install it.

```
~ wget http://librarian.launchpad.net/6615094
  /debootstrap_0.3.3.2ubuntu3_all.deb
~ alien --to-rpm debootstrap_0.3.3.2ubuntu3_all.deb
# rpm -Uvh debootstrap-0.3.3.2-2.noarch.rpm
```

   We now have all the tools needed to bootstrap an Ubuntu Feisty system.

4. Create a directory named `xen-images`. We will create all our guest images in this directory.

```
~ mkdir /home/pchaganti/xen-images
```

You can create virtual machines on a local file, a NFS system, a LVM group, or iSCSI storage. To keep things simple, in this chapter we are going to create all our virtual machines in files. The performance is slower, but we are going to focus on the steps needed to create virtual machines without needing to deal with storage techniques. Chapter 6 covers the different storage options available to us when creating virtual machines using Xen.

5. Create three files, one for holding the root file system,/, one for the `/boot`, and the other for the `swap`.

```
~ dd if=/dev/zero of=/home/pchaganti/xen-images/ubuntu_feisty_domU.
  img bs=1G count=6
~ dd if=/dev/zero of=/home/pchaganti/xen-images/ubuntu_feisty_swap_
  domU.img bs=1G count=1
~ dd if=/dev/zero of=/home/pchaganti/xen-images/ubuntu_feisty_boot_
  domU.img bs=1k count=1000
```

6. Create an ext3 filesystem on the root file image. This will be the image where / will be mounted.

```
~ /sbin/mkfs.ext3 /home/pchaganti/xen-
  images/ubuntu_feisty_domU.img
```

7. Create an ext3 filesystem on the boot image file and create swap on the swap file.

```
~ /sbin/mkfs.ext3 /home/pchaganti/xen-images/
  ubuntu_feisty_boot_domU.img
~ /sbin/mkswap /home/pchaganti/xen-
  images/ubuntu_feisty_swap_domU.img
```

We need to mount these files in a directory so that we can read and write in them.

8. Create a directory called `xen-mounts`. We will create directories here for mounting the various file images.

```
~ mkdir -p /home/pchaganti/xen-mounts/ubuntu_feisty_domU
```

9. Mount the file that will be used to store the root file system using a loop back.

```
# mount -o loop /home/pchaganti/xen-images/ubuntu_feisty_domU.img/
  home/pchaganti /xen-mounts/ubuntu_feisty_domU
```

10. Run *debootstrap*. This will download and extract all the necessary files to the above mounted directory.

```
~ /usr/sbin/debootstrap --arch i386 feisty /home/pchaganti/
  xen-mount/ubuntu_feisty_domU  http://archive.ubuntu.com/ubuntu
```

11. We will be using the domU kernel that we created earlier for booting this domain. So this domain will need the kernel modules compiled for that kernel. Copy them from the `/lib/modules` directory.

```
~ mkdir -p xen-mounts/ubuntu_feisty_domU/lib/modules
~ cp -dpR /lib/modules/2.6.16.38-xenU /home/pchaganti/xen-mounts/
  ubuntu_feisty_domU/lib/modules
```

12. Now `chroot` into this new system and configure it.

```
~ chroot xen-mounts/ubuntu_feisty_domU
```

13. Set the hostname for this system.

```
~ echo "ubuntu_fesity_domU" > /etc/hostname
```

14. Set up the filesystems that will be loaded on boot.

```
cat > /etc/fstab << "EOF"
# file system    mount point   type    options           dump pass
/dev/sda1         /             ext3    defaults            0    1
/dev/sda2         /boot         ext3    ro,nosuid,nodev     0    2
/dev/sda3         none          swap    sw                  0    0
proc             /proc         proc    defaults            0    0
sys              /sys          sysfs   defaults            0    0
EOF
```

15. Set up the network. We will be using the loopback interface and `eth0` for the Ethernet connection. The `eth0` interface will be using DHCP to set itself up automatically.

```
cat > /etc/network/interfaces << "EOF"
# The loopback network interface
auto lo
iface lo inet loopback
# The primary network interface
auto eth0
iface eth0 inet dhcp
EOF
```

16. Add a user, create an admin group, and put the added user in this group. Also set the root password.

```
# adduser pchaganti
# addgroup --system admin
# adduser pchaganti admin
# passwd root
```

17. Ubuntu uses `sudo` to let users perform administrative functions. Use `visudo` to edit the `sudoers` file.

```
visudo
# Members of the admin group may gain root privileges
%admin ALL=(ALL) ALL
```

18. We have completed the initial configuration. Exit out of the `chroot` environment and unmount the file system.

```
#exit
#umount /xen-mounts/ubuntu_feisty_domU
```

19. Create the configuration file that will be used by dom0 to create this guest domain. The MAC address used below is an offset of the MAC set block that was allocated to Xen Source, Inc. This is an OUI (Organizationally Unique Identifier) and you can view the entire list online at `http://standards.ieee.org/regauth/oui/oui.txt`.

```
cat > /home/pchaganti/xen-images/ubuntu_feisty_domU.cfg << "EOF"
kernel = "/boot/vmlinuz-2.6.16.38-xenU"
memory = 256
name = "ubuntu_feisty_domU"
disk = ['tap:aio:/home/pchaganti/xen-
  images/ubuntu_feisty_domU.img,sda1,w','tap:aio:/home/pchaganti
  /xen-images/ubuntu_feisty_boot_domU.img,sda2,w','tap:aio:/home
  /pchaganti/xen-images/ubuntu_feisty_swap.img,sda3,w']
vif = [ 'mac=00:16:3e:00:00:10, bridge=xenbr0' ]
root = "/dev/sda1 ro"
EOF
```

20. Call `xm` to create the virtual machine.

```
# xm create /home/pchaganti/xen-images/debian_etch_domU.cfg -c
```

This will start up a console and boot our brand new virtual machine. The usual Linux start up messages will flash by and then you will be staring at the Ubuntu Feisty login prompt. Welcome to your first Xen domU!

```
 * Loading kernel modules...                                                  *
 Loading manual drivers...                                    [ OK ]
 * Activating swap...                                         [ OK ]
 * Checking root file system...                                             fs
ck 1.40-WIP (14-Nov-2006)
/dev/sda1: clean, 11637/768544 files, 112024/1536000 blocks
                                                              [ OK ]
 * Checking file systems...                                                 fs
ck 1.40-WIP (14-Nov-2006)
/dev/sda2: clean, 11/25688 files, 8914/102400 blocks
                                                              [ OK ]
 * Mounting local filesystems...                              [ OK ]
 * Activating swapfile swap...                                [ OK ]
 * Configuring network interfaces...                          [ OK ]
 * Setting up console font and keymap...                      [ OK ]
 * Starting system log daemon...                              [ OK ]
                                                                     *
Starting kernel log...                                        [ OK ]
                                                                     *
Running local boot scripts (/etc/rc.local)                    [ OK ]

Ubuntu feisty (development branch) ubuntu_feisty_domU tty1

ubuntu_feisty_domU login:
```

You can see the running domains by using `xm`.

```
# xm list
```

You can shut down the domain in two different ways—by using the `halt` command inside the domain itself or by calling `xm` to shutdown.

```
# xm shutdown ubuntu_feisty_domU
```

You can disconnect a running domainU from the console using the keyboard shortcut—*Ctrl]*.

You can connect back to this domU by using `xm` and providing the name of the domain you want to connect as a parameter:

```
# xm console ubuntu_feisty_domU
```

You can configure it so that guest domain starts automatically when the server boots up by creating a symbolic link in the `/etc/xen/auto` directory pointing to the configuration file that we created earlier.

What Just Happened?

We created three file images—one for mounting `/boot`, one for the `swap`, and one for the / root directory using the `dd` command. We also created the ext3 file system on the boot and root file images. Linux provides the concept of a loop device that enables you to access a file like a normal device. We used this concept to mount the file on a normal directory on Linux so that we can manipulate the contents of that directory using any normal Linux commands.

Debootstrap is a great command line tool for creating a Debian base system from scratch. It does not have any dependencies on the Debian package system. It works by downloading the `.deb` files for the specified architecture and distribution from a mirror site, and then unpacks the `.deb` files onto the file system into the specified directory. Once it has finished its magic, you have a minimal Debian root file system that you can `chroot` into and finish the configuration. This tool is not usually available as a part of the Red Hat based systems such as the Fedora Core 6. So in order to use *debootstrap* on Fedora Core, we utilized another great tool called *alien*, which makes it easy to convert LSB, Red Hat, Stampede and Slackware packages into Debian packages. Once these packages from various formats have been converted into the Debian format, we can easily install the package using the Debian package management tool—*dpkg*. Since we are running in Fedora, we used *alien* to convert the *debootstrap* deb package into a native format rpm package, which was finally installed on to our Fedora Core 6 system using *dpkg*.

In this chapter we are using files for storing the guest domains. This is the quickest way to get up and running, but is not recommended for production scenarios as the performance of file backed storage is slower than block based storage using disk partitions or LVM. We export these file images as file based VBD in the configuration file for the domain. There are two steps involved in mounting a file on a normal directory:

- First the file image is associated with a loop device that is a special Linux device.
- This loop device is then mounted on a directory on the file system.

We mount the `ubuntu_feisty_domU.img` file on to the specified directory by specifying the option to use a loop device to the `mount` command.

```
mount -o loop /home/pchaganti/xen-images/ubuntu_feisty_domU.img/
              home/pchaganti /xen-mounts/ubuntu_feisty_domU
```

Now we can read and write in this directory just like any other directory in the file system. When we are done working with the directory, we just `umount` the directory from the loop device. We execute the `debootstrap` command, which will download the files for the specified arch for Ubuntu Feisty and populate the specified directory with the minimal file system required for a Ubuntu system. We will need a kernel and kernel modules for booting this minimal Ubuntu system, and for this we will use the domU kernel that we built earlier in this chapter. We copy the kernel modules to the `/lib/modules` directory in the Ubuntu system so that they are available when the kernel boots up this domain. For the current process, `chroot` command modifies the root directory to the specified directory and in effect creates a sandbox. Once you execute `chroot` and your root directory has been modified, all the commands that you execute from that point will operate inside that sandbox environment and you will not have any access to directories or files outside the root directory. We `chroot` into the Ubuntu minimal system that we have just created, and configure the system by setting up the host name, networking, and security options. Once we are done, we exit the `chroot` to get back into our normal environment.

We have an Ubuntu Feisty system all ready to go and now need to tell Xen to create a guest domain to run it. In order to do this we need to create a Xen configuration file that is just a Python file containing directives to be used by `xm` to create the domain. The minimum information that we need to provide for creating a domain is:

- **kernel**: The path to the kernel that will be used for booting the domain.
- **memory**: The amount of memory in MB that will be allocated to this domain.
- **name**: A unique name for the domain. This is the name that will appear in the list of running Xen domains when we use the `xm` command to list the current Xen environment.
- **disk**: A description of the disk that will be used for the domain. The `tap:aio` qualifier for a Virtual Block Device (VBD) indicates that a file system image will be use for exporting to the VBD. This block device can either be a virtual disk or a virtual partition.
- **root**: The parameters for the device that contains the root filesystem.
- **vif**: This defines the Virtual Ethernet Interface (VIF). By default xend will select a random MAC address that will change every time you reboot that domain. If you always want to use a specific MAC address for the domain, you can provide the `mac` option to the `vif` configuration directive. We will explore the various networking related options available in Chapter 5.

This information is specified in a configuration file and is provided as a parameter to the `xm` command to create the domain.

```
xm create /home/pchaganti/xen-images/ ubuntu_feisty_domU .cfg -c
```

This starts up a domain running the Ubuntu Feisty system. `xm` is a command line tool that provides a wide variety of options and parameters and can be used to control and manage most aspects of Xen domains. We are going to look into all the bells and whistles provided by `xm` in the next chapter. We can use this bootstrapping method to install any guest domains that are based on Debian. If we want to install Debian, all the steps will be the same except that when we initially run *debootstrap*, we modify the parameters to specify Debian etch.

```
debootstrap --arch i686 etch /home/pchaganti/xen-
    mounts/debian_etch_domU http://ftp.us.debian.org/debian
```

NetBSD

NetBSD is a secure and highly portable Unix like operating system that runs on a wide variety of platforms—from 64 bit servers to embedded devices (`http://netbsd.org/`). It provides binary emulation for applications built on other platforms, and can thus run most binaries built on Linux without any modification or recompilation. The recent versions of NetBSD starting with version 3.0 provide native support for Xen. We are going to install the latest released version 3.1 in a guest domain.

Time for Action—Install NetBSD

Let's get started installing NetBSD 3.1 in a guest domain.

The NetBSD distribution provides two Xen enabled kernels for NetBSD—one for running the installation, and the other for actually running the NetBSD operating system.

1. Download these files first.

   ```
   ~ wget ftp://ftp.netbsd.org/pub/NetBSD/NetBSD-
      3.1/i386/binary/kernel/netbsd-*XEN3_DOMU.gz
   ```

   ```
   ~ zcat netbsd-INSTALL_XEN3_DOMU.gz > /boot/netbsd-
      INSTALL_XEN3_DOMU
   ```

   ```
   ~ zcat netbsd-XEN3_DOMU.gz > /boot/netbsd-XEN3_DOMU
   ```

2. Create a file image that will be used for storing our NetBSD guest domain.

   ```
   # dd if=/dev/zero of=/home/pchaganti/xen-images/
           netbsd_domU.img bs=1M count=300
   ```

3. Create the Xen configuration file that will be used to start up the NetBSD domU.

   ```
   cat > /home/pchaganti/xen-images/netbsd_domU.cfg << "EOF"
   kernel = "/boot/netbsd-INSTALL_XEN3_DOMU"
   memory = 64
   name = "netbsd_domU"
   disk = ['tap:aio:/home/pchaganti/xen-images
     /netbsd_domU.img,sda1,w', 'tap:aio:/home/pchaganti/xen-
     images/netbsd_swap.img,sda2,w']
   vif = [ 'mac=00:16:3e:00:00:12, bridge=xenbr0' ]
   EOF
   ```

4. Create the domU using `xm`.

   ```
   xm create /home/pchaganti/xen-images/netbsd_domU.cfg -c
   ```

This will start a console with the NetBSD installation.

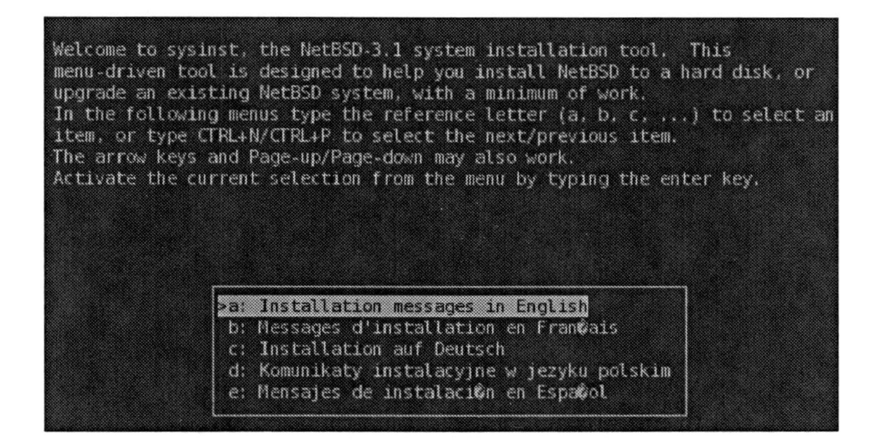

5. Select the option to install to the hard disk.

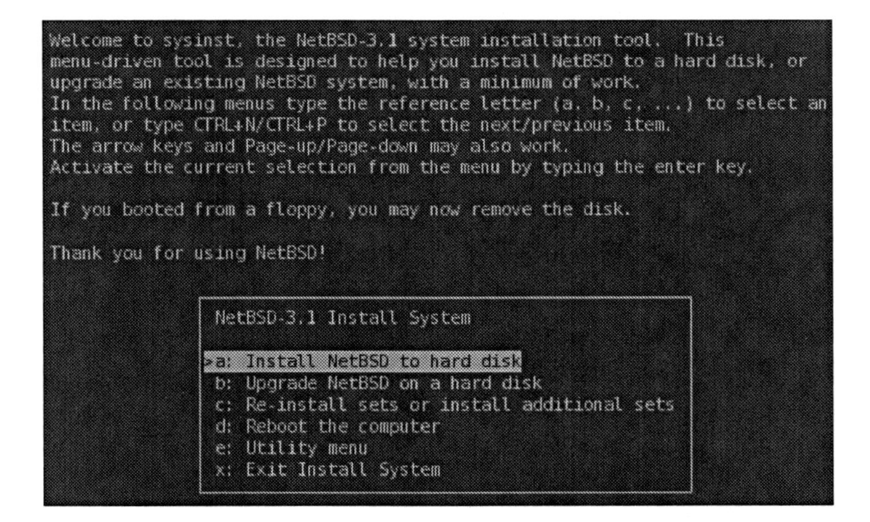

6. Go through the installation using the instructions provided in the NetBSD documentation:

   `http://www.netbsd.org/guide/en/chap-exinst.html`

7. Select the minimum set of packages for installation because the file image we are using as the backing store is only 300 MB. If you want to install a bigger set of packages, please ensure that you increase the size of the file that we created earlier.

8. Once the installation is finished, there are still some configuration related things to be done. So do not reboot. Select the option to go to the **Utility menu**.

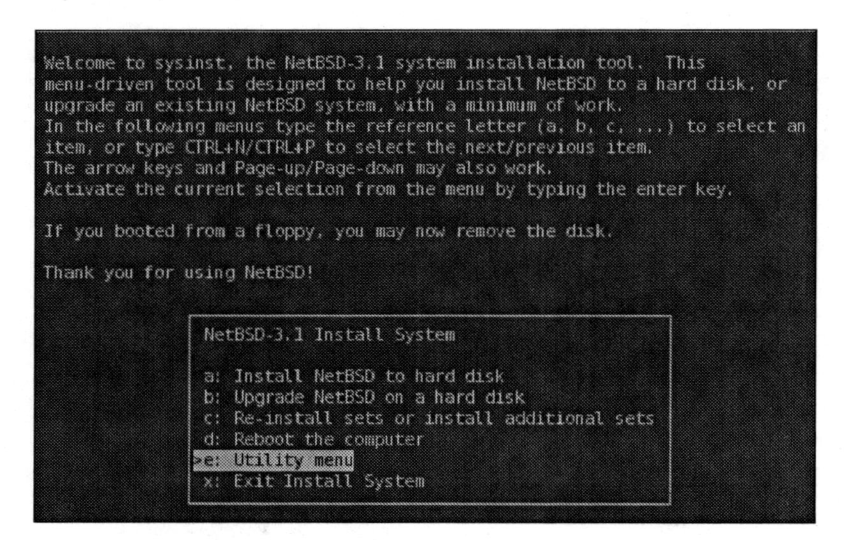

9. In the utility menu select the option to go the shell.

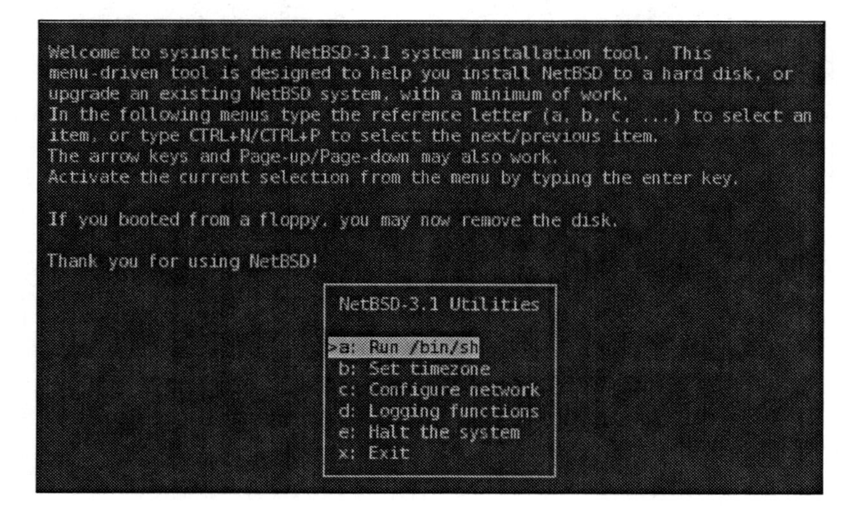

10. Copy the special device files that are used by NetBSD.

```
# mount /dev/xbd0a /mnt
# cp -pR /dev/rxbd* /mnt/dev
# cp -pR /dev/xbd* /mnt/dev
```

11. NetBSD provides access to only one console for the guest. In `Edit /etc/ttys`, turn off all the terminals except `console`.

```
console "/usr/libexec/getty Pc"         vt100   on  secure
ttyE0   "/usr/libexec/getty Pc"         vt220   off secure
ttyE1   "/usr/libexec/getty Pc"         vt220   off secure
ttyE2   "/usr/libexec/getty Pc"         vt220   off secure
ttyE3   "/usr/libexec/getty Pc"         vt220   off secure
```

12. Similarly comment out all the screens in `/etc/wscons.conf`.

```
#screen 0       -       vt100
#screen 1       -       vt100
#screen 2       -       vt100
#screen 3       -       vt100
#screen 4       -       -
#screen 4       80x25bf vt100
```

13. Shut down the install.

```
# halt -p
```

14. Modify the domain configuration file in order to use the standard NetBSD domU kernel instead of the installation kernel.

```
kernel = "/boot/netbsd-XEN3_DOMU"
```

15. Reboot the domain using the domU netbsd kernel:

```
# xm create /home/pchaganti/xen-images/netbsd_domU.cfg -c
```

This will boot you to the NetBSD prompt. Login with the username and password you set as a part of the install.

```
wsconscfg: Cannot open `/dev/ttyEcfg': Device not configured
wsconscfg: Cannot open `/dev/ttyEcfg': Device not configured
Starting syslogd.
Checking for core dump...
Mounting all filesystems...
Clearing /tmp.
Creating a.out runtime link editor directory cache.
Checking quotas: done.
Starting virecover.
Starting local daemons:.
Updating motd.
sendmail: /etc/mail/aliases.db not present, generating
/etc/mail/aliases: 22 aliases, longest 10 bytes, 246 bytes total
Starting sendmail.
Starting inetd.
Starting cron.
Sat Mar 31 08:17:26 EDT 2007
Mar 31 08:17:28  getty[399]: /dev/ttyE3: Device not configured
Mar 31 08:17:28  getty[397]: /dev/ttyE1: Device not configured
Mar 31 08:17:28  getty[387]: /dev/ttyE2: Device not configured

NetBSD/i386 (.) (console)

login: 
```

What Just Happened?

We installed NetBSD the system to a file image by using the install kernel and following the NetBSD installation documentation. We then modified and configured the NetBSD system. Finally we booted the guest domain using the kernel provided.

NetBSD also provides support for creating a Xen dom0. Recent changes in NetBSD provide the additional tools needed to run unmodified guest domains under a NetBSD dom0, using Intel VT-x or AMD VMX extensions. So we could potentially run a NetBSD dom0 and create guest domains under it that run Linux, NetBSD, and Windows.

The NetBSD release currently provides two xenified kernels:

- **netbsd-INSTALL_XEN3_DOMU**: A kernel that can be used to start the NetBSD installation. We used this kernel only for the installation.
- **netbsd-XEN3_DOMU**: A kernel that can be used for booting a NetBSD instance. We used this kernel for booting our guest domain.

CentOS

CentOS is an Enterprise-class Linux Distribution derived from sources provided by RedHat (`http://centos.org/`). It tracks the RedHat Enterprise Linux distribution without any proprietary drivers, is completely free and is hence widely used as a server platform. The installation media for the CentOS is a cd or dvd. We will install the CentOS 4.4 server version. The paravirtualised Xen does not support booting guest domains from a cd-rom or an iso file. So we are going to use another open-source emulator called QEMU (`http://fabrice.bellard.free.fr/qemu/`) to boot the CentOS cd and install into a qemu image. We are then going to take this image and use Xen to create a CentOS virtual machine that runs off the qemu image. We could avoid using qemu if we were running Xen on hardware that supports HVM, such as the Intel VT and AMD Pacifica chipsets. The following chipsets are available on these processors:

- Intel VT
    - Pentium 4 662 and 672
    - Pentium 4 Extreme Edition 955 and 965
    - Xeon MP 7000 series
    - Xeon 3xxx/5xxx/7xxx
    - Pentium D 9x0
    - Intel Core Duo mobile
    - Intel Core 2 Duo processors (excluding the T5200, T5500, E4x00, E2xx0)

- AMD Pacifica
    - Athlon 64
    - Athlon 64 X2
    - Athlon 64 FX
    - Opteron
    - Sempron
    - Phenom
    - Phenom X4
    - Phenom X3
    - Phenom X2

Time for Action—Using qemu to Create a CentOS Image

We will install CentOS by using the iso image for the 4.4 version of the CentOS server.

1. Download the iso image from the mirror closest to you. `http://mirror.linux.duke.edu/pub/centos/4.4/isos/i386/CentOS-4.4.ServerCD-i386.iso`

   We are going to use a VNC to connect to the install screen in `qemu`. If your system does not have it, please install a VNC viewer first (`http://www.tightvnc.com/`). Most distributions provide VNC support out of the box. Install qemu, which will be used for the actual installation.

   ```
   # yum install qemu vnc
   ```

2. Create a qemu file image that we will use for our installation.

   ```
   ~ qemu-img create centos_domU.img 2G
   ```

3. Start `qemu` with the following parameters to make it boot the CentOS server installation cd.

   ```
   ~ qemu -no-kqemu -hda /home/pchaganti/xen-images/centos_domU.img -
   cdrom /home/pchaganti/CentOS-4.4.ServerCD-i386.iso -boot d -vnc 2
   ```

4. Use the `vncviewer` to connect to the display specified in the options provided to `qemu` in the above step. In my case the IP address of my Xen server is 192.168.1.186. This is how I connect to the display with the qemu screen.

   ```
   ~ vncviewer 192.168.1.186:2
   ```

5. The installation screen for CentOS will be displayed as shown in the following screenshot:

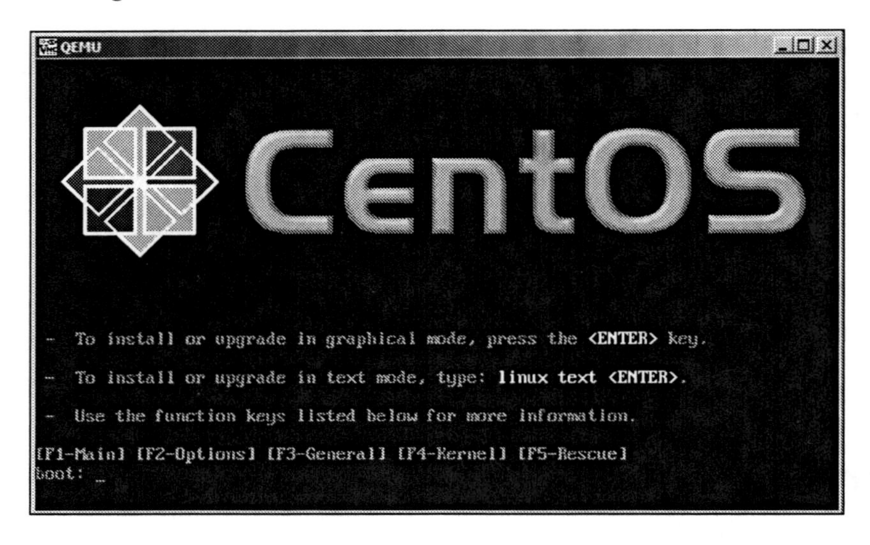

6. Go through the CentOS install following the documentation from the manual.

   http://www.centos.org/docs/4/html/rhel-ig-x8664-multi-en-4/ch-guimode.html

7. Once the installation is complete, select the **Reboot**. This will shutdown your qemu session and take you back to the command prompt.

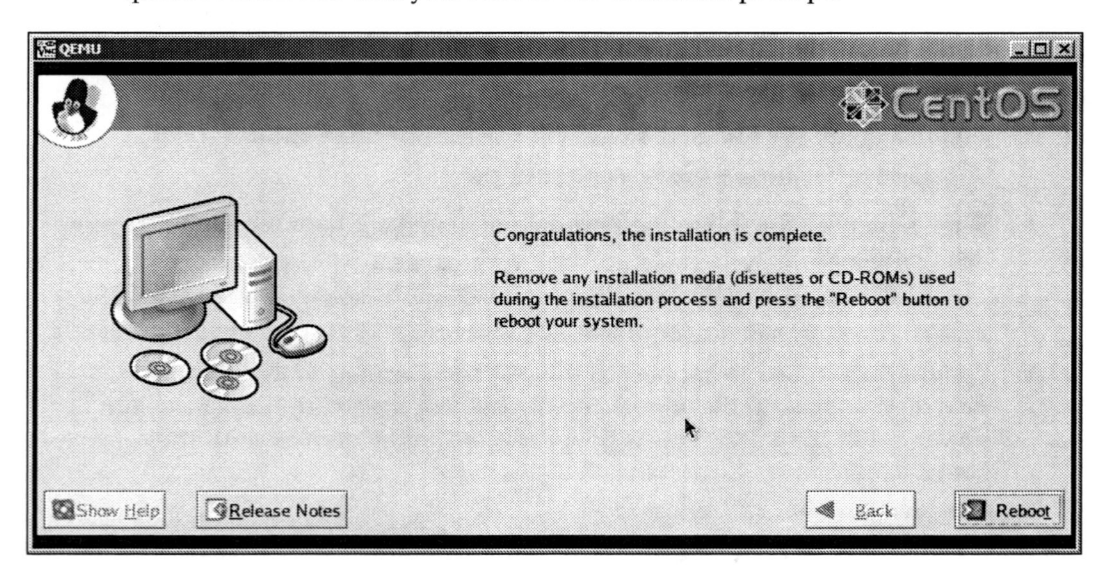

We have completed the installation of CentOS into a qemu image. Please note that this process using `qemu` can be quite slow. Before creating a configuration file for our domU, we need to mount the partitions created inside the qemu image, so that Xen can have access to them. Mount the qemu image on a loopback device first.

```
# losetup /dev/loop1 /home/pchaganti/xen-images/centos_domU.img
```

8. List the partitions that are inside the image. We will need this information later when we try to mount each individual partition inside this image onto a separate directory so that Xen can access it.

```
# fdisk -lu /dev/loop1
```

```
[root@gandalf xen-images]# fdisk -lu /dev/loop1

Disk /dev/loop1: 2147 MB, 2147483648 bytes
255 heads, 63 sectors/track, 261 cylinders, total 4194304 sectors
Units = sectors of 1 * 512 = 512 bytes

      Device Boot      Start         End      Blocks   Id  System
/dev/loop1p1   *          63      208844      104391   83  Linux
/dev/loop1p2          208845     1253069      522112+  82  Linux swap / Solaris
/dev/loop1p3         1253070     4192964     1469947+  83  Linux
[root@gandalf xen-images]#
```

9. Disassociate the image from the loopback device.

```
# losetup -d /dev/loop1
```

10. Create the directories that we will use to mount the partitions from the qemu file image.

```
~ mkdir -p /home/pchaganti/xen-mounts/centos_domU/boot_partition
~ mkdir -p /home/pchaganti/xen-mounts/centos_domU/root_partition
```

11. Mount the partitions on separate directories.

```
# lomount -t ext3 -diskimage /home/pchaganti/xen-
    images/centos_domU.img -partition 1  /home/pchaganti/xen-
    mounts/centos_domU/boot_partition
```

12. Copy the kernel modules to the domU.

```
~ cp -dpR /lib/modules/2.6.16.38-xenU /home/pchaganti/xen-
  mounts/centos_domU/root_partition/lib/modules/
```

13. `chroot` into the domU partition and rename the directory containing the tls libraries.

```
# chroot /home/pchaganti/xen-mounts/centos_domU/root_partition
    /bin/bash
# mv /lib/tls /lib/tls.disabled
```

14. Create the configuration file for starting the CentOS domU.

```
cat > /home/pchaganti/xen-images/centos_domU.cfg << "EOF"
kernel = "/boot/vmlinuz-2.6.16.38-xenU"
ramdisk = "/boot/initrd-2.6.16.38-xenU.img"
memory = 256
name = "centos-domU"
disk = ['tap:aio:/dev/loop1,hda1,w','tap:aio:/dev/loop2,hda3,w']
vif = [ 'mac=00:16:3e:00:00:16, bridge=xenbr0' ]
root = "/dev/hda3 ro"
EOF
```

15. Create the CentOS domU.

```
# xm create /home/pchaganti/xen-images/centos_domU.cfg -c
```

The following screenshot shows the CentOS server booting up as a domU.

```
CentOS release 4.4 (Final)
Kernel 2.6.16.38-xenU on an i686

centos-domU login:
```

What Just Happened?

In this section we used an iso image that contains the CentOS installer. This presents some unique challenges when operating in a paravirtualized environment as Xen cannot boot domains from a cd-rom. If we had been in a Xen HVM environment, it would have been trivial to boot a domain using a CD or an iso image. The work around for this in a paravirtualized environment is to use QEMU—an open-source processor emulator. We created a qemu disk image and then installed CentOS onto that disk image. Qemu allows us to redirect the output from the VGVA display via a VNC session. When `qemu` is used to boot up the CentOS installation CD, the output from that session is exported via VNC, so that we can connect to the display using a VNC viewer and go through the installation. Once the installation is complete the qemu disk image will contain the partitions created in the install process containing the CentOS 4.4 server. We need access to these partitions inside the qemu image so that we can export them to Xen as file backed VBDs, which Xen can access while creating the guest domain. To do this, we use the loop device to mount each partition inside the qemu image on a separate directory. We then create the configuration file for the CentOS guest domain and start it up.

Slackware

Slackware is the oldest Linux distribution still active and prides itself as being the most "unix-like" Linux distribution (`http://www.slackware.com`). We are going to install the latest version of Slackware—11.0 into a guest domain. So far we have been creating Xen domU images from scratch. Doing this gives us a good overview of the various steps that are involved in creating a guest domain, so that we can roll our own when needed. However, you can also download and use ready to go Xen images from several sites on the Internet. These are great time savers as long as the images available meet your needs. We are going to take advantage of readily available Slackware 11.0 Xen images from the jailtime website (`http://jailtime.org/`) and use then for our guest domain.

Time for Action—Utilize Xen Images from jailtime.org

We are going to download and install the complete Slackware Xen image.

1. Download the image from jailtime.

```
~ wget
http://jailtime.org/lib/exe/fetch.php?cache=cache&media=
download%3Aslackware%3Aslackware.11-0.20061220.img.tar.bz2
```

2. Untar the file into our xen-images directory.

```
~ tar -C /home/pchaganti/xen-images -jxvf  slackware.11-
    0.20061220.ig.tar.bz2
```

3. Create a directory for mounting the image.

```
~ mkdir -p /home/pchaganti/xen-mounts/slackware_domU
```

4. Mount the image and copy the kernel modules for the domU kernel. Once the copy is complete, unmount the image.

```
# mount -o loop /home/pchaganti/xen-images/slackware.11-0.img
 /home/pchaganti/xen-mounts/slackware_domU
# cp -dpR /lib/modules/2.6.16.38-xenU /home/pchaganti/xen-
 mounts/slackware_domU/lib/modules/
# umount /home/pchaganti/xen-mounts/slackware_domU/
```

5. Modify the domU configuration file to suit our installation.

```
kernel = "/boot/vmlinuz-2.6.16.38-xenU"
memory = 128
name = "slackware.11-0"
vif = [ 'mac=00:16:3e:00:00:14, bridge=xenbr0' ]
```

```
disk = ['tap:aio:/home/pchaganti/xen-images/slackware.11-
0.img,sda1,w','tap:aio:/home/pchaganti/xen-
images/slackware.swap,sda2,w']
root = "/dev/sda1 ro"
```

6. Create the slackware guest domain.

```
# xm create /home/pchaganti/xen-images/slackware.11-0.xen3.cfg -c
```

The following screenshot shows the slackware domU after start up.

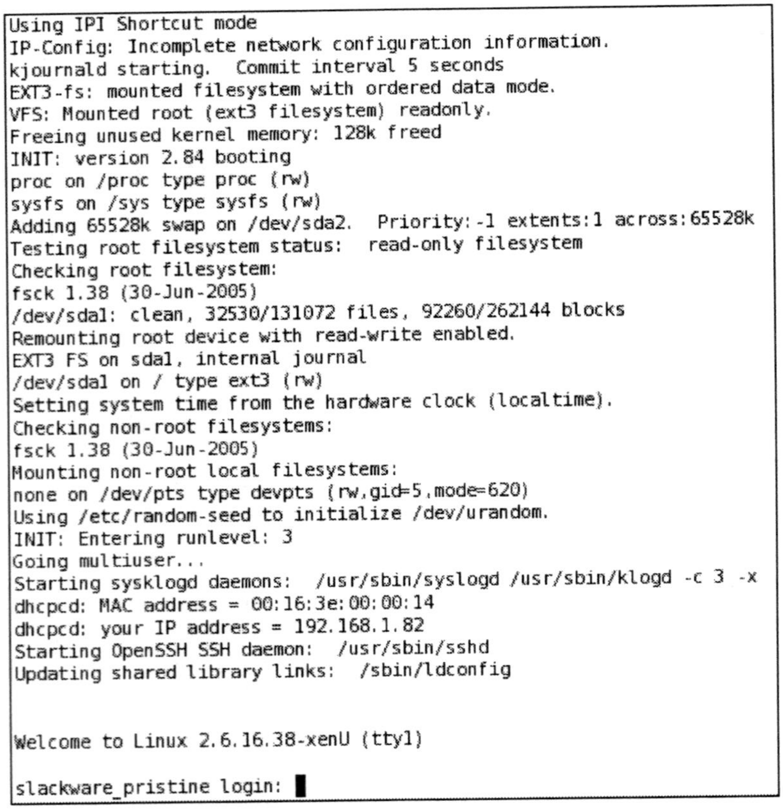

```
Using IPI Shortcut mode
IP-Config: Incomplete network configuration information.
kjournald starting.  Commit interval 5 seconds
EXT3-fs: mounted filesystem with ordered data mode.
VFS: Mounted root (ext3 filesystem) readonly.
Freeing unused kernel memory: 128k freed
INIT: version 2.84 booting
proc on /proc type proc (rw)
sysfs on /sys type sysfs (rw)
Adding 65528k swap on /dev/sda2.  Priority:-1 extents:1 across:65528k
Testing root filesystem status:  read-only filesystem
Checking root filesystem:
fsck 1.38 (30-Jun-2005)
/dev/sda1: clean, 32530/131072 files, 92260/262144 blocks
Remounting root device with read-write enabled.
EXT3 FS on sda1, internal journal
/dev/sda1 on / type ext3 (rw)
Setting system time from the hardware clock (localtime).
Checking non-root filesystems:
fsck 1.38 (30-Jun-2005)
Mounting non-root local filesystems:
none on /dev/pts type devpts (rw,gid=5,mode=620)
Using /etc/random-seed to initialize /dev/urandom.
INIT: Entering runlevel: 3
Going multiuser...
Starting sysklogd daemons:  /usr/sbin/syslogd /usr/sbin/klogd -c 3 -x
dhcpcd: MAC address = 00:16:3e:00:00:14
dhcpcd: your IP address = 192.168.1.82
Starting OpenSSH SSH daemon:  /usr/sbin/sshd
Updating shared library links:  /sbin/ldconfig


Welcome to Linux 2.6.16.38-xenU (tty1)

slackware_pristine login:
```

What Just Happened?

Creating Xen guest domains from scratch is time consuming and there are times when we just need to do some quick testing and really don't want to configure a whole new domain. There are several sites on the Internet that offer complete Xen images that can be used out of the box. You can find domains that contain complete operating systems or Xen images that contain an operating system configured for a particular application.

`jailtime.org` provides complete Xen images for several operating systems. The slackware.11-0.21220.img.tar.bz2 file that we have downloaded contains the following:

- Slackware.11-0.img (the slackware root file system image)
- Slackware.11-0.xen2.cfg (configuration for Xen 2)
- Slackware.11-0.xen3.cfg (configuration for Xen 3)
- Slackware.11-0.swap (swap file)

The images contain everything we need, so all we have to do is ensure that the configuration matches what we want and create the guest domain.

Summary

In this chapter we created several different virtual machines or domUs that run different operating systems. We installed each of these domUs using different installation methods, so we could get a feel for the various different ways of creating guest domains in Xen.

- We created an Ubuntu Feisty domU using the *debootstrap* tool for bootstrapping an Ubuntu install from scratch.
- We created a NetBSD domain using an install image and the kernel image provided as a part of the NetBSD distribution.
- We created a CentOS 4.4 server guest domain using `qemu` to install to a disk image, mounted the partitions from that disk image onto file system directories and used those directories to boot our CentOS 4.4 server from Xen.
- We used a readily available Xen domU image from jailtime to create a Slackware domain.

In the next chapter, we will explore the Xen management tools, `xm` and `xend`.

4

Managing Xen

We successfully created several Xen guest domains in the last chapter. In this chapter, we will explore the different tools that are available to manage Xen and the Xen domains. The first tool that we will explore is the Xen Manager (xm), which ships as a part of the Xen distribution. This enables you to perform various administrative and management tasks through the command line. We will also look at two other third party tools—XenMan and Virt-Manager—which are graphical applications for managing Xen.

We will explore the following tools for managing Xen:

- xm
- XenMan
- virt-manager

Xen Domain Configuration Files

The domain configuration file for a Xen domain specifies the various parameters that govern the behavior of the domain. The various files related to configuring Xen are located in the `/etc/xen` directory. The configuration file, which contains various options in the `key=value` format is an executable file written in Python. The options must therefore be in valid Python code. The `/etc/xen/xend-config.sxp` is a special configuration file that is used for creating dom0.

The configuration files for the domUs that you are creating can be placed anywhere as long as you provide the full path to the file when creating the domain. The `/etc/xen/auto` is a special directory and any domain configuration files that are placed in this directory will automatically be started when the `xend` daemon starts.

Here are some of the common options specified in a Xen domain configuration file:

- **kernel**: The kernel image that is used for the domain is provided as the complete path to the kernel image file.
- **ramdisk**: Specifies the initial ramdisk for the domain. If your kernel has built-in drivers for your root file system and hard disk, you may not need to create and specify a ramdisk. This is provided as a complete path to the location of the `initrd` file.
- **memory**: Specifies the amount of RAM, in megabytes, that is allocated for the domain. Insufficient memory allocation will prevent the domain from starting up. You must also ensure that the total memory taken by Xen—both dom0 and all the domUs—must be less than or equal to the amount of physical RAM present in your machine.
- **name**: Provides a unique name to identify the domain. This name will be be displayed when you list the domains running on the system.
- **root**: Specifies the root device for the domain.
- **disk**: Specifies a list of block devices that is exported to the domain. This is provided in the following the format:

  ```
  disk = [ "backend device", "frontend device", "mode" ]
  ```

  The "`backend device`" specifies the format and name of the device that will be exported to the guest domain. The format can be a simple file image or an actual physical disk. A file image is exported to the guest domain as a file-based VBD by Xen. This is the format that we will use in this chapter as it is the simplest and quickest way to get started with Xen. In Chapter 6 we will look at other forms of storage for Xen domains:

  - `file://path_to_the_file_image`: The file image is exported as a loopback device. The setup of the loopback device is taken care of by Xen.
  - `tap:aio:/path_to_the_file_image`: The file image is exported as a tap device that can be accessed by the Xen blktap driver. This is specified as the suggested way in the Xen documentation for exporting file images to the guest domain.
  - `phy:device:/name_of_the_device`: The specified physical device is exported to the guest domain. The device can be specified in the usual `/dev/sda1` form or using the hex major/minor number for the device—`0x301`.

The `"frontend device"` specifies how the exported `backend device` should appear to the guest domain. This can be specified in the usual `/dev/sda1` form or using the hex major/minor number for the device—`0x301`.

The "`mode`" specifies whether the device is to be exported as read-only or read-write. The two valid options are:

  - **r**—read-only
  - **rw**—read and write.

- **vif**: Specifies the virtual network interface configuration for the domain. This is provided in the following format:

```
vif = [ "key1 = value1", "key2 = value2" ]
```

  The common options used for this configuration directive are:

  - **bridge**: Specifies the network bridge that will be used for this interface.
  - **mac**: Specifies the MAC address for this virtual interface. If you do not provide a MAC address, it is set to a random MAC address by Xen on boot. The random address is selected from the range of addresses assigned to Xensource by IEEE in the XenSource Organizationally Unique Identifier (OUI) range 00-16-3E. You can also use this directive for defining a static MAC address that will receive a static IP assignment from your DHCP server.

- **on_reboot**: Specifies the action taken by the domain during a reboot. The valid states on a reboot are:
  - **destroy**: Completely shuts down the domain.
  - **preserve**: The domain is not cleaned up. The debugging information from the domain is available to help debug crashes.
  - **rename-restart**: The old domain is not cleaned up. Instead it is renamed and a new domain is started in place of the old domain.
- **on_crash**: Specifies the action taken by the domU if it crashes. The valid states for this directive are the same as that for on_reboot option.
- **vcpus**: The number of virtual CPUs.

The following figure shows the domain configuration file that we used in the previous chapter for creating and running the Ubuntu Feisty guest domain:

```
ubuntu_feisty_domU.cfg
kernel = "/boot/vmlinuz-2.6.16.38-xenU"

memory = 128

name = "ubuntu_feisty_domU"

disk = ['tap:aio:/home/pchaganti/xen-images/
ubuntu_feisty_domU.img,sda1,w','tap:aio:/home/pchaganti/xen-images/
ubuntu_feisty_boot_domU.img,sda2,w']

vif = [ 'mac=00:16:3e:00:00:13, bridge=xenbr0' ]

root = "/dev/sda1 ro"
```

The above screenshot provides an example of some of the parameters and configuration directives that we have been discussing in this section.

Xen Management User Interface—xm

xm is a management tool that communicates with the Xen hypervisor through xend—the Xen daemon. Running xm commands requires administrative privileges on the system as it uses the privileged communication channel between xend and the Hypervisor. xm is also designed to perform its functions in an asynchronous way.

Executing an xm command will immediately return to the caller, but the actual operation may not be complete. Some of the domain commands may actually take quite a long time to complete. The only way to determine whether the command is successfully completed is to print out the list periodically and check it. The two most fundamental operations that we use xm for are to create a domain and to list the state of all the domains in the current Xen environment. The state field in the list of domains has one of the five possible states for a domain:

- **r—running**: Lists domains currently active on a CPU.
- **b—blocked**: Lists domains that are blocked. This happens when the vcpu is waiting for an external event to happen for this domain.
- **p—paused**: Lists domains that are suspended. The paused domain will still consumes allocated resources such as memory, but is not eligible for scheduling by the Xen hypervisor.
- **s—shutdown**: Lists domains that are in process of shutting down.
- **c—crashed**: Lists domains that are crashed.

The normal listing of domains is in a table format that is not very easy for other tools to parse. therefore `xm` also provides a `-long` option to list the domain information in an S-Expression format that can be easily parsed by other tools.

Time for Action—Xen Manager

You need not install `xm` separately. On Fedora Core, installing Xen will include the installation of various Xen tools. We have already used `xm` in the previous chapter to create domains and list the domains. We will now demonstrate some of the common tasks performed with `xm`.

1. Print a list of the running domains in the current Xen environment.

   # xm list

```
[root@gandalf ~]# xm list
Name                                      ID  Mem VCPUs      State   Time(s)
Domain-0                                   0  129     1     r-----   29584.9
ubuntu_feisty_domU                        15  256     1     -b----       4.0
[root@gandalf ~]#
```

2. Print detailed information about the dom0 in the current Xen environment.

   # xm list Domain-0 -long

```
[root@gandalf ~]# xm list --long Domain-0
(domain
    (domid 0)
    (on_crash restart)
    (memory 128)
    (uuid 00000000-0000-0000-0000-000000000000)
    (bootloader_args )
    (name Domain-0)
    (maxmem 128)
    (on_reboot restart)
    (on_poweroff destroy)
    (vcpus 1)
    (bootloader )
    (shadow_memory 0)
    (cpu_weight 256)
    (cpu_cap 0)
    (features )
    (on_xend_start ignore)
    (on_xend_stop ignore)
    (cpu_time 29586.0096388)
    (online_vcpus 1)
    (status 2)
    (memory_dynamic_min 129)
    (memory_dynamic_max 0)
    (state r-----)
)
[root@gandalf ~]#
```

3. Print detailed information about a domain in the current Xen environment. The listing is quite long and is therefore broken up into the following two screenshots.

```
# xm list --long centos-domU
```

```
[root@gandalf ~]# xm list --long ubuntu_feisty_domU
(domain
    (domid 15)
    (on_crash restart)
    (memory 256)
    (uuid 6bd2061f-0329-c381-0559-3b6ae4b27cde)
    (bootloader_args )
    (name ubuntu_feisty_domU)
    (maxmem 256)
    (on_reboot restart)
    (on_poweroff destroy)
    (localtime 0)
    (vcpus 1)
    (bootloader )
    (shadow_memory 0)
    (cpu_weight 256)
    (cpu_cap 0)
    (features )
    (on_xend_start ignore)
    (on_xend_stop ignore)
    (start_time 1176827222.72)
    (cpu_time 3.969989542)
    (online_vcpus 1)
    (image
        (linux
            (kernel /boot/vmlinuz-2.6.16.38-xenU)
            (args 'root=/dev/sda1 ro ')
            (root '/dev/sda1 ro')
        )
    )
    (status 2)
    (memory_dynamic_min 256)
    (memory_dynamic_max 256)
    (state -b----)
    (store_mfn 5183)
    (console_mfn 5182)
    (device
        (vif
            (bridge xenbr0)
            (mac 00:16:3e:00:00:13)
            (script vif-bridge)
            (uuid eac104b0-bf4a-8a52-b802-e6b68ec416c5)
            (backend 0)
        )
    )
```

```
    (device
        (vbd
            (uname file:/home/pchaganti/xen-images/ubuntu_feisty_domU.img)
            (uuid 6925ae91-7b42-3852-5a2a-5746b8e97c08)
            (mode w)
            (dev sda1:disk)
            (backend 0)
        )
    )
    (device
        (vbd
            (uname file:/home/pchaganti/xen-images/ubuntu_feisty_boot_domU.img)
            (uuid d91530e3-1b08-df95-5196-bd2dacd8cf49)
            (mode w)
            (dev sda2:disk)
            (backend 0)
        )
    )
)
```

4. Pause a running domU in the current Xen environment.

   `# xm pause ubuntu_feisty_domU`

   ◦ List the domains to make sure it has paused:

     `# xm list`

```
[root@gandalf ~]# xm list
Name                                        ID   Mem VCPUs      State   Time(s)
Domain-0                                     0   129     1     r-----   29593.6
ubuntu_feisty_domU                          15   256     1     --p---       4.0
[root@gandalf ~]#
```

5. Unpause the previously paused domU:

   `# xm unpause ubuntu_feisty_domU`

   ◦ List the domains to make sure the domain has been unpaused.

     `# xm list`

```
[root@gandalf ~]# xm list
Name                                        ID   Mem VCPUs      State   Time(s)
Domain-0                                     0   129     1     r-----   29594.7
ubuntu_feisty_domU                          15   256     1     -b----       4.0
[root@gandalf ~]#
```

6. Save the state of a running domU in the current Xen environment to the specified file. The following will save the state to the disk file and remove it from the list of running domains.

   `# xm save ubuntu_feisty_domU feisty.save`

- List the domains to make sure the saved domain is no longer displayed in the list of running domains:

  # xm list

```
[root@gandalf ~]# xm list
Name                                      ID  Mem VCPUs      State   Time(s)
Domain-0                                   0  129     1     r-----   29841.8
[root@gandalf ~]#
```

7. Restore a domain from the saved state. This will restore the domain from the file with the state information and put the domain back in a running state.

   # xm restore feisty.save

   - List the domains to make sure the domain is once again displayed in the list of running domains:

     # xm list

```
[root@gandalf ~]# xm list
Name                                      ID  Mem VCPUs      State   Time(s)
Domain-0                                   0  129     1     r-----   30095.3
ubuntu_feisty_domU                        16  256     1     -b----       0.0
[root@gandalf ~]#
```

8. Check the Xen kernel buffer messages. The following screenshot shows a partial listing from my machine.

   # xm dmesg

```
[root@gandalf ~]# xm dmesg

 http://www.cl.cam.ac.uk/netos/xen
 University of Cambridge Computer Laboratory

 Xen version 3.0.4-1 (root@) (gcc version 4.1.1 20070105 (Red Hat 4.1.1-51)) Fri Mar 30 22:46:36 EDT 2007
 Latest ChangeSet: Thu Feb 15 11:34:58 2007 +0000 13139:3341afbb1953

(XEN) Command line: /xen.gz noreboot dom0_mem=128M
(XEN) Physical RAM map:
(XEN)  0000000000000000 - 000000000009f800 (usable)
(XEN)  000000000009f800 - 00000000000a0000 (reserved)
(XEN)  00000000000f0000 - 0000000000100000 (reserved)
(XEN)  0000000000100000 - 000000001bef0000 (usable)
(XEN)  000000001bef0000 - 000000001bef3000 (ACPI NVS)
(XEN)  000000001bef3000 - 000000001bf00000 (ACPI data)
(XEN)  00000000e0000000 - 00000000f0000000 (reserved)
(XEN)  00000000fec00000 - 0000000100000000 (reserved)
(XEN) System RAM: 446MB (457276kB)
(XEN) ACPI: RSDP (v000 HP-CPC                                ) @ 0x000f85a0
(XEN) ACPI: RSDT (v001 HP-CPC AWRDACPI 0x42302e31 AWRD 0x00000000) @ 0x1bef3040
(XEN) ACPI: FADT (v002 HP-CPC AWRDACPI 0x42302e31 AWRD 0x00000000) @ 0x1bef30c0
(XEN) ACPI: SSDT (v001 HP-CPC POWERNOW 0x00000001  LTP 0x00000001) @ 0x1bef6d80
(XEN) ACPI: SRAT (v001 HP-CPC HAMMER   0x00000001 AMD  0x00000001) @ 0x1bef6ec0
(XEN) ACPI: MCFG (v001 HP-CPC AWRDACPI 0x42302e31 AWRD 0x00000000) @ 0x1bef6fc0
(XEN) ACPI: MADT (v001 HP-CPC AWRDACPI 0x42302e31 AWRD 0x00000000) @ 0x1bef6cc0
(XEN) ACPI: DSDT (v001 HP-CPC AWRDACPI 0x00001000 MSFT 0x0100000e) @ 0x00000000
(XEN) NUMA turned off
(XEN) Faking a node at 0000000000000000-000000001bef0000
(XEN) Domain heap initialised: DMA width 30 bits
(XEN) Xen heap: 10MB (10384kB)
(XEN) PAE disabled.
(XEN) found SMP MP-table at 000f4680
(XEN) DMI 2.4 present.
(XEN) Using APIC driver default
(XEN) ACPI: Local APIC address 0xfee00000
(XEN) ACPI: LAPIC (acpi_id[0x00] lapic_id[0x00] enabled)
(XEN) Processor #0 15:15 APIC version 16
(XEN) ACPI: LAPIC (acpi_id[0x01] lapic_id[0x01] disabled)
(XEN) ACPI: LAPIC_NMI (acpi_id[0x00] high edge lint[0x1])
(XEN) ACPI: LAPIC_NMI (acpi_id[0x01] high edge lint[0x1])
(XEN) ACPI: IOAPIC (id[0x02] address[0xfec00000] gsi_base[0])
(XEN) IOAPIC[0]: apic_id 2, version 33, address 0xfec00000, GSI 0-23
(XEN) ACPI: INT_SRC_OVR (bus 0 bus_irq 0 global_irq 2 dfl dfl)
(XEN) ACPI: INT_SRC_OVR (bus 0 bus_irq 9 global_irq 21 low level)
(XEN) ACPI: IRQ0 used by override.
```

9. Print the host information for the current Xen environment.

   # xm info

```
[root@gandalf ~]# xm info
host                   : gandalf
release                : 2.6.16.38-xen0
version                : #4 Fri Mar 30 06:22:51 EDT 2007
machine                : i686
nr_cpus                : 1
nr_nodes               : 1
sockets_per_node       : 1
cores_per_socket       : 1
threads_per_core       : 1
cpu_mhz                : 1989
hw_caps                : 078bfbff:e3d3fbff:00000000:00000010:00000001:00000001:00000001
total_memory           : 446
free_memory            : 44
xen_major              : 3
xen_minor              : 0
xen_extra              : .4-1
xen_caps               : xen-3.0-x86_32
xen_pagesize           : 4096
platform_params        : virt_start=0xfc000000
xen_changeset          : Thu Feb 15 11:34:58 2007 +0000 13139:3341afbb1953
cc_compiler            : gcc version 4.1.1 20070105 (Red Hat 4.1.1-51)
cc_compile_by          : root
cc_compile_domain      :
cc_compile_date        : Fri Mar 30 22:46:36 EDT 2007
xend_config_format     : 3
[root@gandalf ~]#
```

10. Print the Xen log. The following screenshot shows a partial listing from the Xen log on my machine.

    # xm log

```
[2007-03-30 04:56:31 xend 3158] INFO (SrvDaemon:283) Xend Daemon started
[2007-03-30 04:56:31 xend 3158] INFO (SrvDaemon:287) Xend changeset: Thu Feb 15 11:34:58 2007 +0000 13139:3341afbb1953.
[2007-03-30 04:56:32 xend.XendDomainInfo 3158] DEBUG (XendDomainInfo:212) XendDomainInfo.recreate({\047paused\047: 0, \
047cpu_time\047: 209844740765L, \047ssidref\047: 0, \047handle\047: [0, 0, 0, 0, 0, 0, 0, 0, 0, 0, 0, 0, 0, 0, 0, 0], \
047shutdown_reason\047: 0, \047dying\047: 0, \047dom\047: 0, \047mem_kb\047: 411180, \047maxmem_kb\047: -4, \047max_vcp
u_id\047: 0, \047crashed\047: 0, \047running\047: 1, \047shutdown\047: 0, \047online_vcpus\047: 1, \047blocked\047: 0})
[2007-03-30 04:56:32 xend.XendDomainInfo 3158] INFO (XendDomainInfo:224) Recreating domain 0, UUID 00000000-0000-0000-0
000-000000000000.
[2007-03-30 04:56:32 xend.XendDomainInfo 3158] WARNING (XendDomainInfo:246) No vm path in store for existing domain 0
[2007-03-30 04:56:32 xend.XendDomainInfo 3158] DEBUG (XendDomainInfo:715) Storing VM details: {\047shadow_memory\047: \
0470\047, \047uuid\047: \04700000000-0000-0000-0000-000000000000\047, \047on_reboot\047: \047restart\047, \047on_powero
ff\047: \047destroy\047, \047name\047: \047Domain-0\047, \047xend/restart_count\047: \0470\047, \047vcpus\047: \0471\04
7, \047vcpu_avail\047: \0471\047, \047memory\047: \047402\047, \047on_crash\047: \047restart\047, \047maxmem\047: \0474
02\047}
[2007-03-30 04:56:32 xend.XendDomainInfo 3158] DEBUG (XendDomainInfo:750) Storing domain details: {\047cpu/0/availabili
ty\047: \047online\047, \047memory/target\047: \047411648\047, \047name\047: \047Domain-0\047, \047console/limit\047: \
0471048576\047, \047vm\047: \047/vm/00000000-0000-0000-0000-000000000000\047, \047domid\047: \0470\047}
[2007-03-30 04:56:35 xend 3158] DEBUG (XendDomain:153) number of vcpus to use is 0
[2007-03-30 04:56:36 xend.XendDomainInfo 3158] DEBUG (XendDomainInfo:940) XendDomainInfo.handleShutdownWatch
[2007-03-30 04:56:36 xend 3158] INFO (SrvServer:116) unix path=/var/lib/xend/xend-socket
[2007-03-30 16:28:05 xend 3121] INFO (SrvDaemon:283) Xend Daemon started
[2007-03-30 16:28:06 xend 3121] INFO (SrvDaemon:287) Xend changeset: Thu Feb 15 11:34:58 2007 +0000 13139:3341afbb1953.
[2007-03-30 16:28:07 xend.XendDomainInfo 3121] DEBUG (XendDomainInfo:212) XendDomainInfo.recreate({\047paused\047: 0, \
047cpu_time\047: 218765795815L, \047ssidref\047: 0, \047handle\047: [0, 0, 0, 0, 0, 0, 0, 0, 0, 0, 0, 0, 0, 0, 0, 0], \
047shutdown_reason\047: 0, \047dying\047: 0, \047dom\047: 0, \047mem_kb\047: 411180, \047maxmem_kb\047: -4, \047max_vcp
u_id\047: 0, \047crashed\047: 0, \047running\047: 1, \047shutdown\047: 0, \047online_vcpus\047: 1, \047blocked\047: 0})
[2007-03-30 16:28:07 xend.XendDomainInfo 3121] INFO (XendDomainInfo:224) Recreating domain 0, UUID 00000000-0000-0000-0
000-000000000000.
[2007-03-30 16:28:07 xend.XendDomainInfo 3121] WARNING (XendDomainInfo:246) No vm path in store for existing domain 0
[2007-03-30 16:28:07 xend.XendDomainInfo 3121] DEBUG (XendDomainInfo:715) Storing VM details: {\047shadow_memory\047: \
0470\047, \047uuid\047: \04700000000-0000-0000-0000-000000000000\047, \047on_reboot\047: \047restart\047, \047on_powero
ff\047: \047destroy\047, \047name\047: \047Domain-0\047, \047xend/restart_count\047: \0470\047, \047vcpus\047: \0471\04
7, \047vcpu_avail\047: \0471\047, \047memory\047: \047402\047, \047on_crash\047: \047restart\047, \047maxmem\047: \0474
02\047}
```

11. Monitor the Xen domains in real time similar to the Unix top utility.

    # xm top

```
xentop - 13:15:00   Xen 3.0.4-1
2 domains: 1 running, 1 blocked, 0 paused, 0 crashed, 0 dying, 0 shutdown
Mem: 457276k total, 412156k used, 45120k free    CPUs: 1 @ 1989MHz
      NAME  STATE   CPU(sec) CPU(%)     MEM(k) MEM(%)  MAXMEM(k) MAXMEM(%) VCPUS NETS NETTX(k) NETRX(k) VBDS   VBD_OO   VBD_RD   VBD_WR SSID
  Domain-0 -----r      30213    0.4     131328   28.7   no limit       n/a     1    4  2062439   491292    0        0        0        0    0
ubuntu_feisty_domU --b---        0    0.0     262144   57.3     270336      59.1     1    1        0       75    2        0        0       31    0

 Delay  Networks  vBds  VCPUs  Repeat header  Sort order  Quit
```

12. List all the block devices used by a domain:

    # xm block-list ubuntu_feisty_domU

```
[root@gandalf ~]# xm block-list ubuntu_feisty_domU
Vdev  BE handle state evt-ch ring-ref BE-path
2049    0    0     4     4      8     /local/domain/0/backend/vbd/16/2049
2050    0    0     4     5      9     /local/domain/0/backend/vbd/16/2050
[root@gandalf ~]#
```

13. List all the block devices used by a domain in detail:

    # xm block-list ubuntu_feisty_domU --long

```
[root@gandalf ~]# xm block-list ubuntu_feisty_domU --long
(2049
    ((backend-id 0)
        (virtual-device 2049)
        (device-type disk)
        (state 4)
        (backend /local/domain/0/backend/vbd/16/2049)
        (ring-ref 8)
        (event-channel 4)
    )
)
(2050
    ((backend-id 0)
        (virtual-device 2050)
        (device-type disk)
        (state 4)
        (backend /local/domain/0/backend/vbd/16/2050)
        (ring-ref 9)
        (event-channel 5)
    )
)
[root@gandalf ~]#
```

14. List all the network interfaces used by a domain:

```
# xm network-list ubuntu_feisty_domU
```

```
[root@gandalf ~]# xm network-list ubuntu_feisty_domU
Idx BE     MAC Addr.     handle state evt-ch tx-/rx-ring-ref BE-path
0   0  00:16:3e:00:00:13    0     4      6     523  /522     /local/domain/0/backend/vif/16/0
[root@gandalf ~]#
```

15. List all the network interfaces used by a domain in detail:

```
# xm network-list ubuntu_feisty_domU
```

```
[root@gandalf ~]# xm network-list ubuntu_feisty_domU --long
(0
    ((backend-id 0)
        (mac 00:16:3e:00:00:13)
        (handle 0)
        (state 4)
        (backend /local/domain/0/backend/vif/16/0)
        (tx-ring-ref 523)
        (rx-ring-ref 522)
        (event-channel 6)
        (request-rx-copy 1)
        (feature-rx-notify 1)
        (feature-sg 1)
        (feature-gso-tcpv4 1)
    )
)
[root@gandalf ~]#
```

16. Display the uptime for all the domains in your Xen environment.

```
# xm uptime
```

```
[root@gandalf ~]# xm uptime
Name                                  ID Uptime
Domain-0                               0  3:01:34
ubuntu_feisty_domU                     2  0:12:53
[root@gandalf ~]#
```

17. Reboot a domain. This does not re-read the Xen configuration file for that domain. If you want to reload the configuration for that domain, you need to use a `halt` command followed by a `create` command.

```
# xm reboot ubuntu_feisty_domU
```

18. Suspend a domain:

```
# xm suspend ubuntu_feisty_domU
```

19. Resume a suspended domain:

```
# xm resume ubuntu_feisty_domU
```

20. Rename a running domain:

```
# xm rename ubuntu_feisty_domU prabhakar_domU
```

21. Connect to domain console:

```
# xm console ubuntu_feisty_domU
```

22. Shut down a domain:

```
# xm shutdown ubuntu_feisty_domU
```

What Just Happened?

`xm` is a tool that is provided with the Xen installation. It is the main interface for the management of Xen domains. It is very useful to get comfortable using `xm` as it is guaranteed to be available on any system that is running Xen. In this section we explored the various management tasks that can be performed using `xm`.

`Xm` also provides the ability to perform other management functions that we will cover later in this book:

- **Virtual devices**: Adds and removes virtual devices while the guest domain is running. You can attach and detach both storage devices and network devices using `xm`. We will discuss the network device related commands in the next chapter and the storage device related options in Chapter 6.
- **Security**: Manages security policies in Xen. We will explore Xen security in Chapter 7.
- **Migration**: Migrates the guest domain. We will learn about migration in Chapter 8.

There are also other less common management related operations you can perform with `xm`. Please check the latest Xen documentation or the `xm` manual page for details on these options.

XenMan—Installing and Running

Console applications are not for everyone and some people prefer to click around in a GUI to perform tasks. In this section we are going to use XenMan, a graphical management application for Xen. It is an open-source application and provides a wide range of administrative capabilities.

Time for Action—Install and Run XenMan

XenMan is currently not available in Fedora's yum repositories. We will download it from the website (`http://xenman.sourceforge.net/`) and install it.

1. Download the rpm for Fedora Core from the project site:
   `http://downloads.sourceforge.net/xenman/xenman-0.6-1.fedora.noarch.rpm?modtime=1168052247&big_mirror=0.`
2. Use yum to install the following dependencies:
   - **python-paramiko**: A Python module that implements the SSH2 protocol for secure connections to remote machines.
   - **gmp**: Provides the GNU MP library for arbitrary precision arithmetic, signed integer operations, rational numbers, and floating point numbers.
   - **python-crypto**: A cryptography library for Python that provides a collection of both secure hash functions and encryption algorithms.

   ```
   # yum install python-crypto python-paramiko
   ```
3. Install the downloaded XenMan rpm. It will give information about the missing Fedora Core Xen package as we are not running the Fedora Core 6 version, but the version of Xen compiled from the Xensource mercurial repository. Override and install the rpm:

   ```
   # rpm -i --nodeps xenman-0.6-1.fedora.noarch.rpm
   ```
4. Start the application:

   ```
   $ xenman
   ```
5. Here is the application on startup. The initial screen displays a summary. Select the **localhost** *node to see the summary for the local server:*

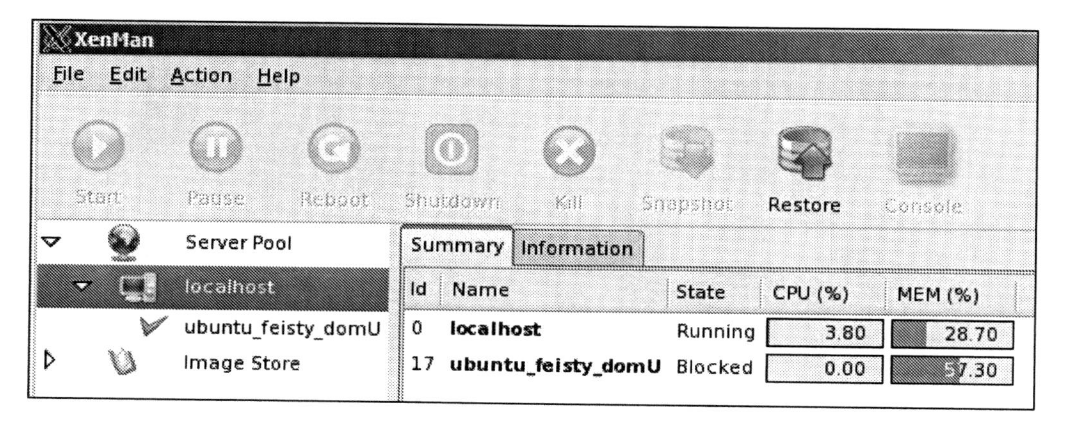

6. XenMan provides a right-click context menu that enables you to perform various management actions.

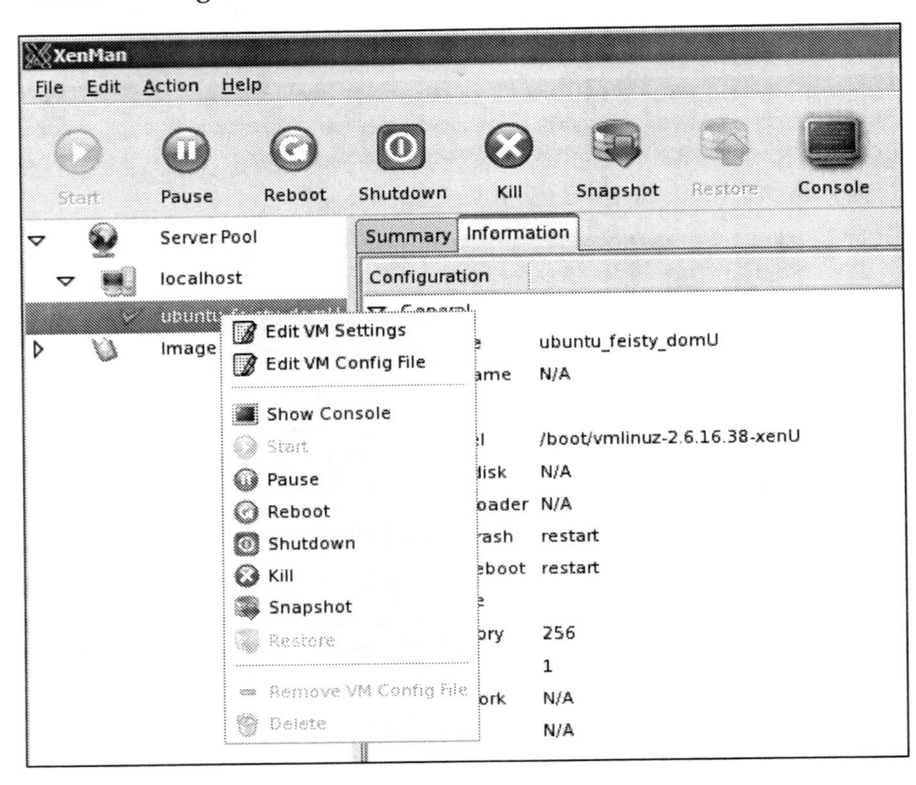

7. Select a domain and choose **Show Console** from the context menu to display the console for the chosen domain.

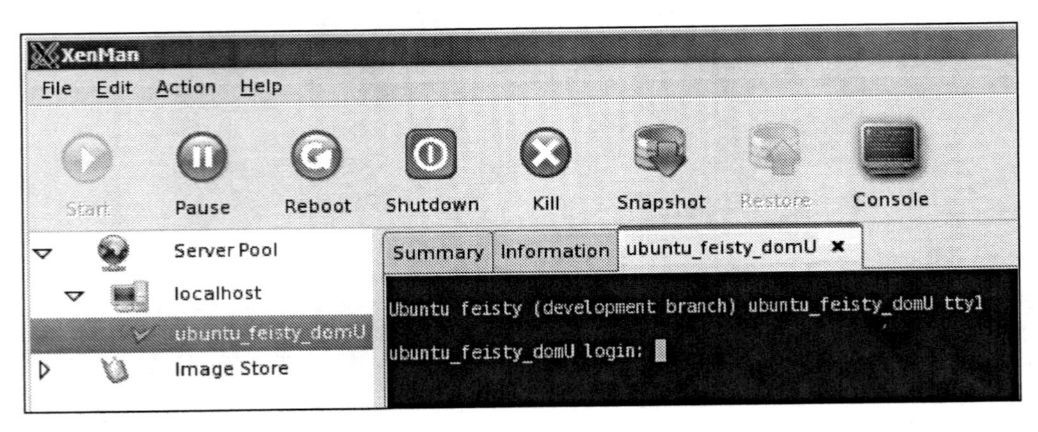

8. Select the **localhost** in the tree view to get more options:

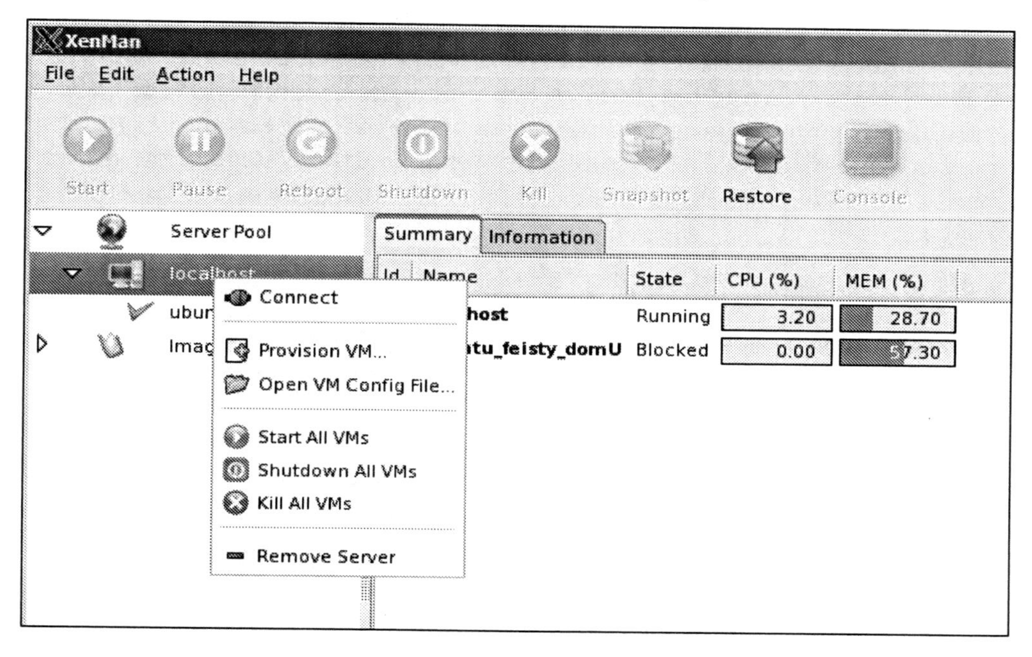

9. Open the domain configuration file by selecting the **Open VM Config File** option from the context menu. This will work only with domain configuration generated by XenMan as it adds a special header to the file.
10. Add a new Xen server to the application by selecting the **Server Pool** node in the tree view and selecting **Add Server** from the context menu.

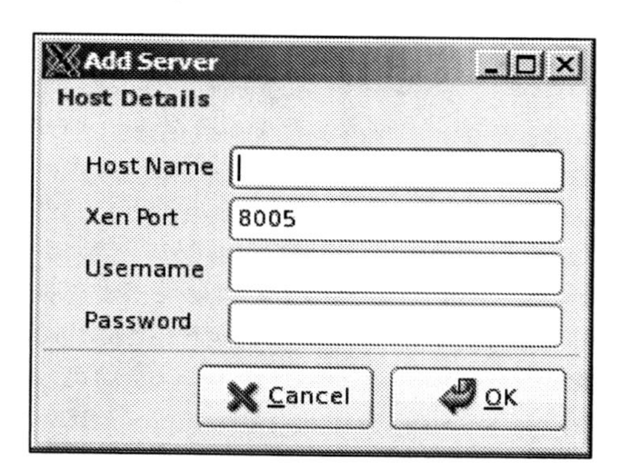

XenMan provides the ability to provision Virtual Machines. Provisioning allows you to create new virtual machines quickly using predefined parameters. We will examine Xen domain provisioning in Chapter 8.

What Just Happened?

XenMan is a fantastic open-source tool that makes managing your Xen servers a breeze. It is under active development and already has a lot of useful features. It is a great way to start getting familiar with using and managing Xen. The GUI interface is simple enough for novices while providing advanced options for more advanced users. The roadmap for XenMan details some of the things that are in the pipeline for future releases (`http://xenman.sourceforge.net/roadmap.html`).

Some of the main advantages of using XenMan are:

- **Consolidated Management**: You can manage all your Xen servers and the guest domains running on them remotely. It provides a dashboard that can give you a quick overview of your entire Xen environment at a glance.
- **Easy Administration**: You can perform most of your common administrative, provisioning, and monitoring tasks directly from the graphical console.
- **Secure access**: XenMan uses the highly secure SSH tunneling for communicating with the remote Xen servers.
- **Provisioning**: It provides a powerful Image Store provisioning SDK so you can define and execute your own Virtual Machine images and provisioning schemes. We will explore the provisioning capabilities of XenMan in Chapter 8.
- **Domain Consoles**: You can connect to the consoles of your local or remote domains easily with one click.

Virtual Machine Manager

The Virtual Machine manager (virt-manager) is another graphical management application for virtual machines. It provides a dashboard view of currently running domains and their statistics. It also contains an embedded VNC client viewer that enables you to connect to a guest domain and display its full graphical console. It also comes with a command line tool called `virt-install` that can be used for provisioning new virtual machines. Virt-manager is intended to be used with any virtualization, not just Xen. However, currently Xen, Qemu, and KVM are the only supported hypervisors. In this section we will install virt-manager and examine its capabilities for managing Xen.

Time for Action—Running virt-manager

virt-manager is an application that is well integrated with the Xen support provided in Fedora Core 6, and is available in the Fedora repositories. Installing Xen in Fedora Core automatically installs virt-manager for you. This means that you will be using Fedora Core's Xen packages instead of Xen compiled from the Xensource mercurial repository. In order to use virt-manager, Fedora Xen packages were installed as the version compiled from the latest source release had trouble working with the latest pre-release versions of Xen.

1. If you don't already have the virt-manager, install it using yum.

```
# yum install virt-manager
```

2. Launch virt-manager to display the connection screen.

```
$ virt-manager
```

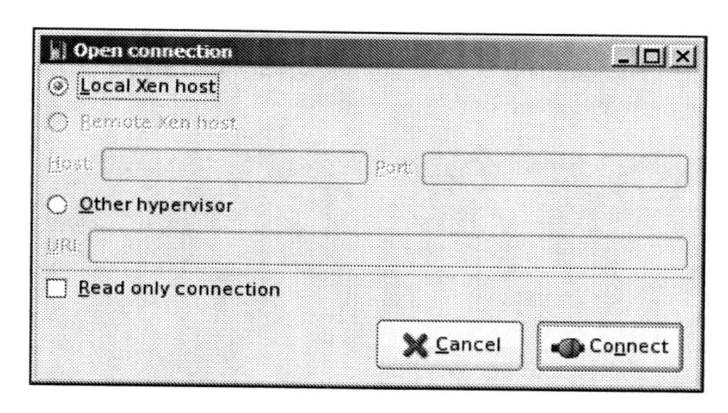

3. Connect to the local Xen host to view a summary of the domains in the Xen environment.

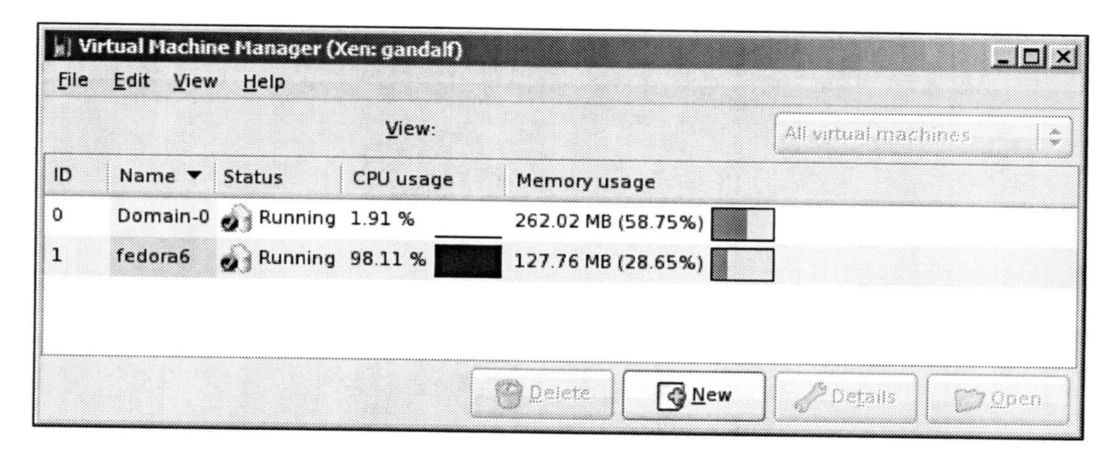

4. Right click a domain and select **Details** to see its properties:

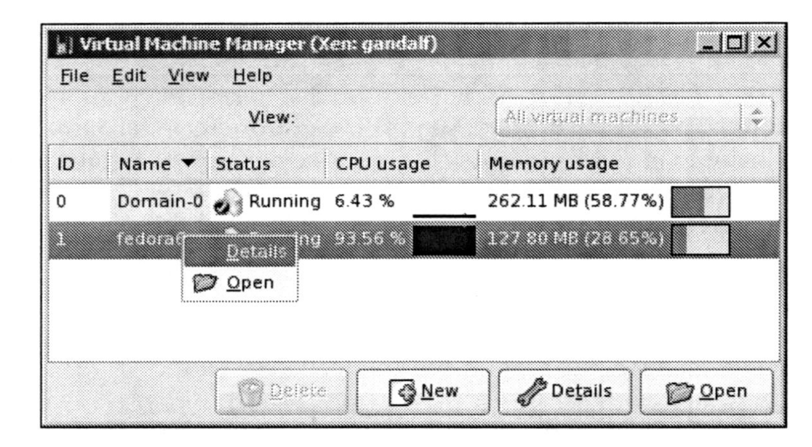

The details screen for a domain has two tabs—**Overview** and **Hardware**. The following screenshot shows the overview screen:

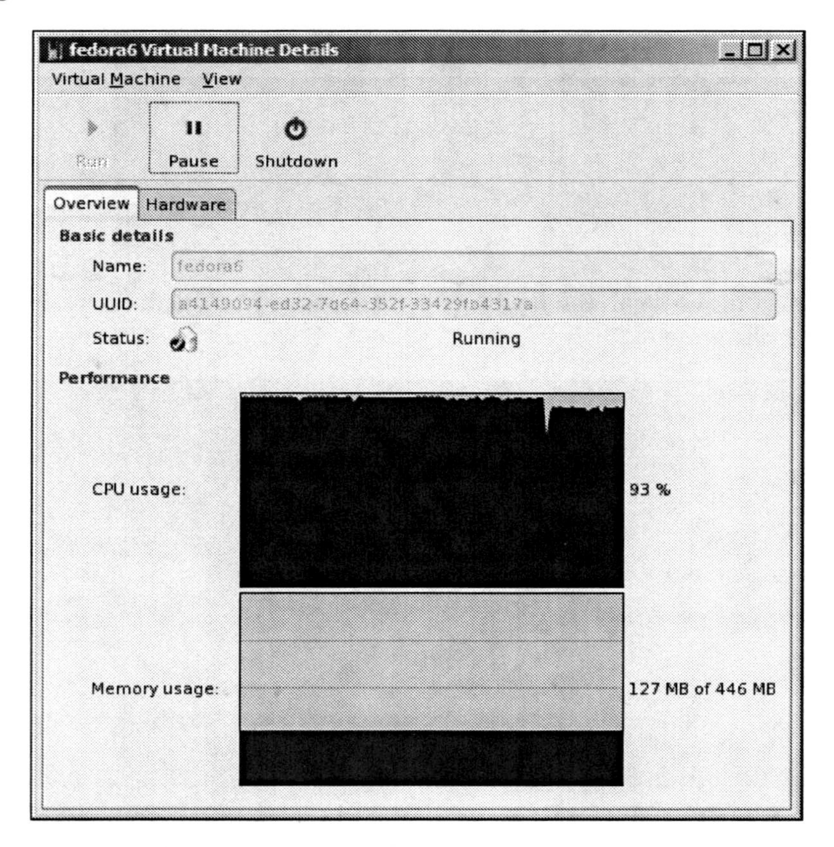

5. Click on the **Hardware** tab to see the hardware details for the selected domain:

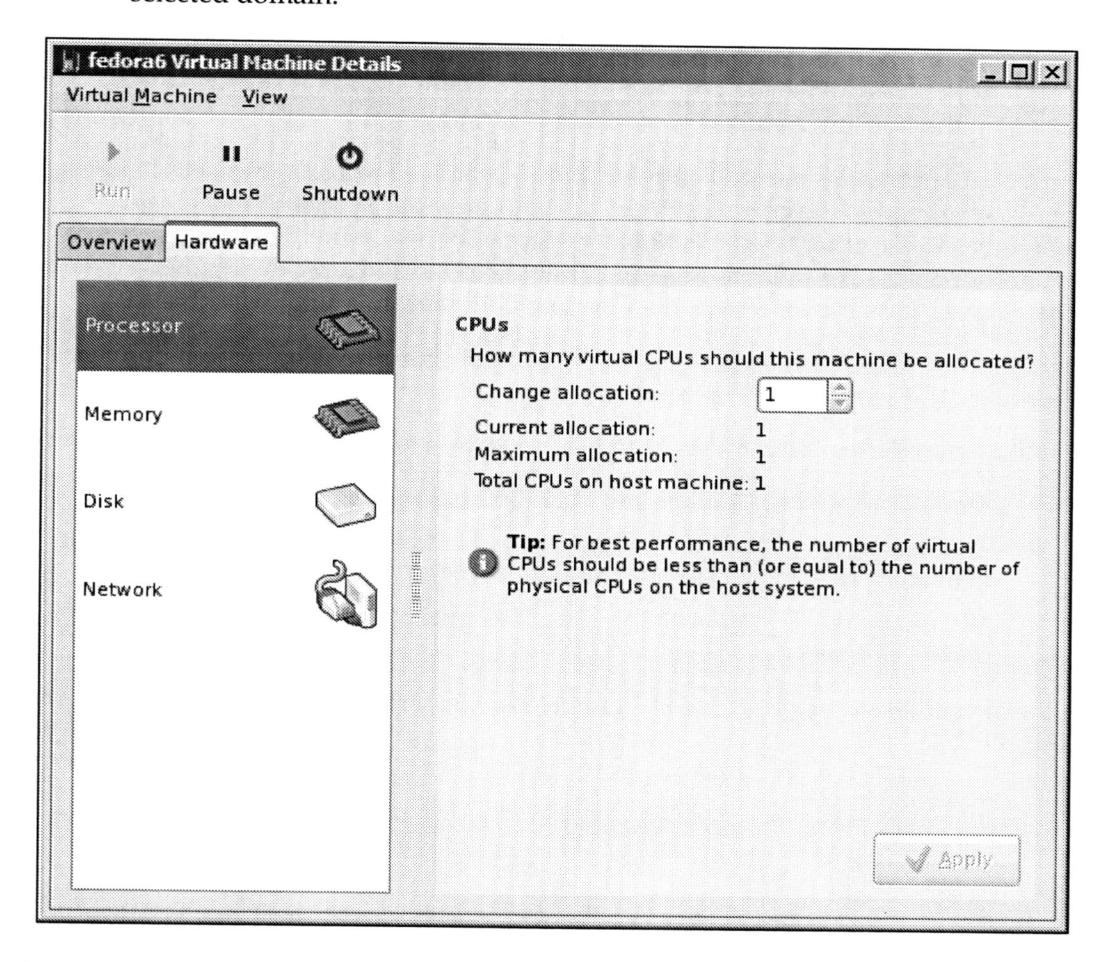

What Just Happened?

virt-manager uses the Python bindings provided by the libvirt project (`http://libvirt.org`) to communicate with the Xen hypervisor. Libvirt provides an API to interface with various hypervisors such as Xen, Qemu, and KVM in a hypervisor independent way. So virt-manager can be used not only with the Xen hypervisor, but also with these other virtualization technologies. It provides a great way to manage your local Xen domains. The virt-install command line tool provided by the virt-manager can be used for provisioning systems, and we will use this tool when will examine the topic of provisioning Xen domains in Chapter 8.

Summary

xm provides a great way to quickly run the administrative and management commands on your Xen server from the command line. It provides a wide variety of options and is available on any Xen installation. However, it is restricted to managing the Xen environment on which it is running.

virt-manager provides a simple graphical user interface for managing Xen domains, but it is restricted to the current server. XenMan provides similar management capabilities to the other two tools but also gives you the option to manage a remote Xen instance. This is a killer feature and really helps administrators who are trying to consolidate their various management responsibilities into a single dashboard.

Both XenMan and Virt-manager provide capabilities for provisioning Xen domains. We will look at the topic of Xen provisioning in Chapter 8.

In this chapter we explored the following options for managing the Xen environment:

- **Xen manager (xm)**: A command line tool that is part of Xen.
- **XenMan**: A graphical administration application that provides the ability to manage both local and remote domains.
- **Virt-manager**: A graphical application for managing the local Xen environment.

In the next chapter, we are going to examine the networking options available when using Xen.

5 Networking

The guest domains we create need to connect with each other and the outside world. Xen provides a couple of different networking options, which we will explore in this chapter:

- Bridged networking
- Routed networking
- Virtual Local Area Network (VLAN) with Network Address Translation (NAT)

It is possible to do more advanced networking configurations with Xen, but in this chapter we will address the above three scenarios. We will use a server with a single Ethernet card running our base Fedora Core 6 system. The default networking on this box is shown in the following diagram. As we go through the various options in this chapter, we will modify this diagram to indicate the changes made to the network interfaces and configuration while using Xen.

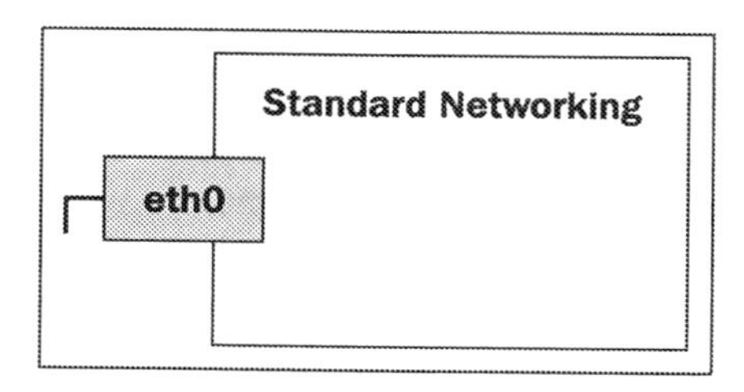

Bridged Networking

Bridging is a technique used for connecting different network segments. It is the default option for Xen networking as it simply connects all the virtual machines to the outside world through virtual network interfaces connected to the bridges created by Xen. Bridges connect two LANs (local area networks) together and forward frames using their MAC (media access control) address. They thus operate at the lowest level of the network layer and are completely unaware of something like an IP. The following diagram depicts a simple network bridge.

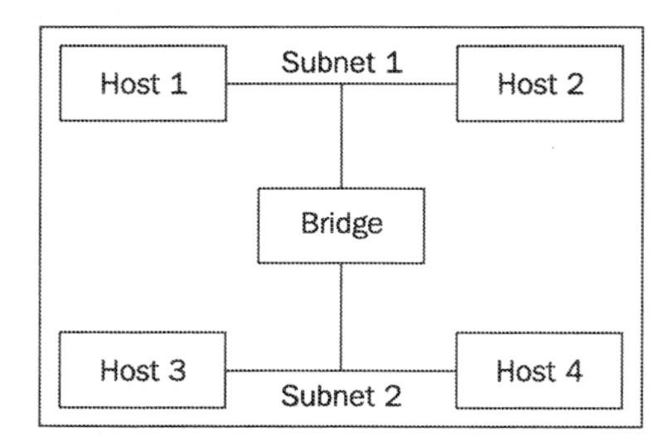

A network bridge is primarily utilized to connect multiple network segments by using the MAC addresses for addressing. It uses broadcasting to locate devices that are not known to it. Once the devices have been located, their MAC addresses are stored in a bridge table, which is the first place checked when a new packet frame comes in.

The most common form of bridging used on Ethernet networks is *transparent bridging*. The systems using the bridge are not aware of its existence as the bridge transparently passes traffic from one network segment to another based on specific MAC addresses. Transparent bridging is standardized by IEEE as 802.1D (`http://www.ieee802.org/1/pages/802.1D-2003.html`). The MAC address `FF:FF:FF:FF:FF:FF` is used as the broadcast address for the both networks. Any Ethernet frames sent to this address are resent to all the ports on that specific network segment. Source addresses on a frame are used to record entries in a table, while destination addresses are used to look up entries and match them to the proper segment to which they are to be sent.

In this section we will look at how Xen actually sets up your network configuration to use bridging.

Time for Action—Using Bridged Networking

We will configure the domU to use bridged networking, and then create a guest domain that uses bridged networking.

1. The default networking setup in Xen is bridged, which can be confirmed by looking at the xend configuration file—`/etc/xen/xend-config.sxp`. It should have the following two lines uncommented in the file:

```
(network-script network-bridge)
  (vif-script vif-bridge)
```

2. Create a new configuration file for the domU. You can use any of the domU images we have created in the earlier chapters or any custom images that you have. Replace settings in this file accordingly for the image you choose. We will use a ttylinux image:

```
kernel = "/boot/vmlinuz-2.6.16.38-xenU"
memory = 32
name = "bridged_domU"
disk = ['tap:aio:/home/pchaganti/xen-
  images/ttylinux_domU.img,hda,w']
vif = [ 'bridge=xenbr0' ]
root = "/dev/hda1 ro"
```

3. Start up the domU by using `xm`:

```
# xm create /home/pchaganti/xenimages/ttylinux_domU.cfg -c
```

4. Check to make sure that the domU is up and running:

```
[root@gandalf xen-images]# xm list
Name                                      ID   Mem VCPUs      State   Time(s)
Domain-0                                   0   129     1     r-----    338.5
bridged_domU                               4    32     1     -b----      0.3
[root@gandalf xen-images]# 
```

What Just Happened?

The default dom0 configuration file—`/etc/xen/xend-config.sxp` is set up to use bridged networking so that all domains appear on the network as individual hosts. This default bridge created by the dom0 on startup is named `xenbr0`. On some older systems it is called `xen-br0`. On the newer Fedora systems, the bridge is actually called `eth0`, and the physical hardware is called `peth0`. In our domU configuration file, we specified that we want to connect the network interface for this domU to the bridge named `xenbr0`.

When using bridged networking, Xen creates a network bridge and then connects the actual physical network interface to this bridge. Virtual network interfaces are then created for dom0 and each of the guest domains; these are all attached to the network bridge. In this manner, all the domains can connect to any address to which the physical network interface can connect.

Let us take a detailed look at what all these different terms mean and what actually happens when your dom0 is set up to use bridged networking and you create a domU that uses that bridge.

Here is the sequence of events that happen when you boot up your Xen server and xend starts up (only dom0 is started and no guest domains set to auto start by xend. I only have one physical network interface on my server and it is named `eth0`).

1. Execute the `/etc/xen/scripts/network-bridge` script.
2. This will create a new network bridge called `xenbr0`.
3. Copy the MAC address and IP address from the physical network interface `eth0`.
4. Stop the physical network interface `eth0`.
5. Create a new pair of connected virtual ethernet interfaces—`veth0` and `vif0.0`.
6. Assign the previously copied MAC address and IP address to the virtual interface `veth0`.
7. Rename the physical network interface to `peth0` from `eth0`.
8. Rename the virtual network interface `veth0` to `eth0`.
9. Attach `peth0` and `vif0.0` to the bridge `xenbr0`.
10. Bring up the bridge `xenbr0`, and the network interfaces `peth0`, `eth0`, and `vif0.0`.

Check the network configuration and list details of the various interfaces created by running the `ifconfig` command:

```
[root@gandalf ~]# ifconfig
eth0      Link encap:Ethernet  HWaddr 00:13:D3:93:20:49
          inet addr:192.168.1.86  Bcast:192.168.1.255  Mask:255.255.255.0
          UP BROADCAST RUNNING MULTICAST  MTU:1500  Metric:1
          RX packets:67327 errors:0 dropped:0 overruns:0 frame:0
          TX packets:56487 errors:0 dropped:0 overruns:0 carrier:0
          collisions:0 txqueuelen:0
          RX bytes:7383835 (7.0 MiB)  TX bytes:24635790 (23.4 MiB)

lo        Link encap:Local Loopback
          inet addr:127.0.0.1  Mask:255.0.0.0
          UP LOOPBACK RUNNING  MTU:16436  Metric:1
          RX packets:103827 errors:0 dropped:0 overruns:0 frame:0
          TX packets:103827 errors:0 dropped:0 overruns:0 carrier:0
          collisions:0 txqueuelen:0
          RX bytes:25696648 (24.5 MiB)  TX bytes:25696648 (24.5 MiB)

peth0     Link encap:Ethernet  HWaddr FE:FF:FF:FF:FF:FF
          UP BROADCAST RUNNING NOARP  MTU:1500  Metric:1
          RX packets:2839621 errors:0 dropped:0 overruns:0 frame:0
          TX packets:60804 errors:0 dropped:0 overruns:0 carrier:0
          collisions:2022 txqueuelen:1000
          RX bytes:1621897194 (1.5 GiB)  TX bytes:25109482 (23.9 MiB)
          Interrupt:16 Base address:0xdd00

vif0.0    Link encap:Ethernet  HWaddr FE:FF:FF:FF:FF:FF
          UP BROADCAST RUNNING NOARP  MTU:1500  Metric:1
          RX packets:56487 errors:0 dropped:0 overruns:0 frame:0
          TX packets:67328 errors:0 dropped:0 overruns:0 carrier:0
          collisions:0 txqueuelen:0
          RX bytes:24635790 (23.4 MiB)  TX bytes:7384078 (7.0 MiB)

xenbr0    Link encap:Ethernet  HWaddr FE:FF:FF:FF:FF:FF
          UP BROADCAST RUNNING NOARP  MTU:1500  Metric:1
          RX packets:11358 errors:0 dropped:0 overruns:0 frame:0
          TX packets:0 errors:0 dropped:0 overruns:0 carrier:0
          collisions:0 txqueuelen:0
          RX bytes:2105206 (2.0 MiB)  TX bytes:0 (0.0 b)

[root@gandalf ~]#
```

The hardware address or MAC address for all the interfaces is set to the broadcast address `FF:FF:FF:FF:FF:FF`. Use the bridge utility tools for listing the Ethernet bridge configuration to examine the topology of the default bridge `xenbr0` created by xend on startup. This will also show the various interfaces or ports attached to each bridge created. As you can see in the following screenshot, the interfaces `peth0` and `vif0.0` are both attached to the bridge `xenbr0`:

```
[root@gandalf ~]# brctl show
bridge name     bridge id               STP enabled     interfaces
xenbr0          8000.feffffffffff       no              peth0
                                                        vif0.0
[root@gandalf ~]#
```

The following diagram shows the network configuration with the various interfaces created and the connections to the bridge when `xend` is started and only dom0 is running.

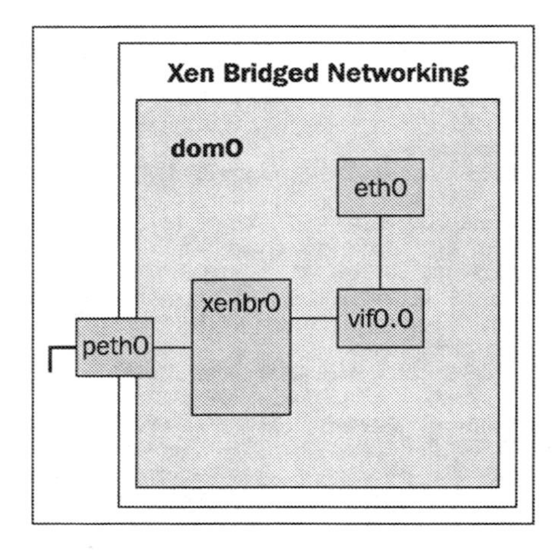

When we start up domU with the configuration file created above, the network configuration looks as follows:

```
[root@gandalf ~]# ifconfig
eth0      Link encap:Ethernet  HWaddr 00:13:D3:93:20:49
          inet addr:192.168.1.86  Bcast:192.168.1.255  Mask:255.255.255.0
          UP BROADCAST RUNNING MULTICAST  MTU:1500  Metric:1
          RX packets:70438 errors:0 dropped:0 overruns:0 frame:0
          TX packets:59554 errors:0 dropped:0 overruns:0 carrier:0
          collisions:0 txqueuelen:0
          RX bytes:7747774 (7.3 MiB)  TX bytes:25713192 (24.5 MiB)

lo        Link encap:Local Loopback
          inet addr:127.0.0.1  Mask:255.0.0.0
          UP LOOPBACK RUNNING  MTU:16436  Metric:1
          RX packets:109966 errors:0 dropped:0 overruns:0 frame:0
          TX packets:109966 errors:0 dropped:0 overruns:0 carrier:0
          collisions:0 txqueuelen:0
          RX bytes:26869820 (25.6 MiB)  TX bytes:26869820 (25.6 MiB)

peth0     Link encap:Ethernet  HWaddr FE:FF:FF:FF:FF:FF
          UP BROADCAST RUNNING NOARP  MTU:1500  Metric:1
          RX packets:2843020 errors:0 dropped:0 overruns:0 frame:0
          TX packets:64051 errors:0 dropped:0 overruns:0 carrier:0
          collisions:2048 txqueuelen:1000
          RX bytes:1622380372 (1.5 GiB)  TX bytes:26201072 (24.9 MiB)
          Interrupt:16 Base address:0xdd00

vif0.0    Link encap:Ethernet  HWaddr FE:FF:FF:FF:FF:FF
          UP BROADCAST RUNNING NOARP  MTU:1500  Metric:1
          RX packets:59555 errors:0 dropped:0 overruns:0 frame:0
          TX packets:70439 errors:0 dropped:0 overruns:0 carrier:0
          collisions:0 txqueuelen:0
          RX bytes:25713586 (24.5 MiB)  TX bytes:7748017 (7.3 MiB)

vif8.0    Link encap:Ethernet  HWaddr FE:FF:FF:FF:FF:FF
          UP BROADCAST RUNNING NOARP  MTU:1500  Metric:1
          RX packets:5 errors:0 dropped:0 overruns:0 frame:0
          TX packets:267 errors:0 dropped:95 overruns:0 carrier:0
          collisions:0 txqueuelen:32
          RX bytes:1256 (1.2 KiB)  TX bytes:93712 (91.5 KiB)

xenbr0    Link encap:Ethernet  HWaddr FE:FF:FF:FF:FF:FF
          UP BROADCAST RUNNING NOARP  MTU:1500  Metric:1
          RX packets:11407 errors:0 dropped:0 overruns:0 frame:0
          TX packets:0 errors:0 dropped:0 overruns:0 carrier:0
          collisions:0 txqueuelen:0
          RX bytes:2121605 (2.0 MiB)  TX bytes:0 (0.0 b)

[root@gandalf ~]#
```

As we can see in the previous screenshot, new interfaces were added to the network configuration. We can examine the bridge configuration to confirm that these new interfaces were correctly attached to the network bridge by using the bridge utils:

```
[root@gandalf ~]# brctl show
bridge name     bridge id               STP enabled     interfaces
xenbr0          8000.feffffffffff       no              vif8.0
                                                        peth0
                                                        vif0.0
[root@gandalf ~]#
```

We can see how a new virtual interface `vif8.0` was attached to the bridge. This interface is used by the domU that we created.

The following diagram shows the complete network configuration with all the created interfaces and the attachments to the bridge, with both dom0 and domU running.

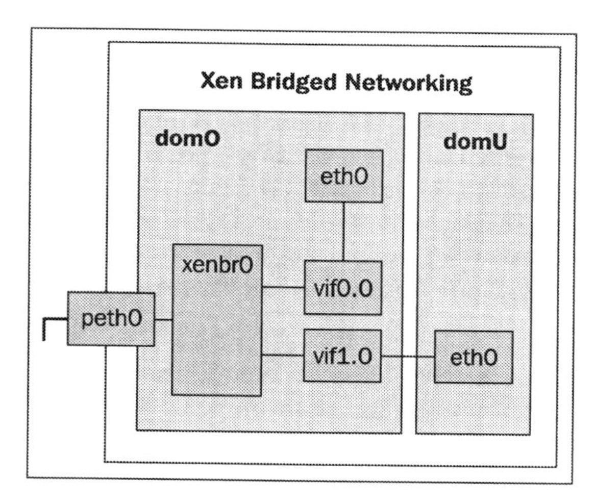

Routed Networking

Routing is a technique that uses IP forwarding to relay network traffic from one segment to another. In this case, dom0 in Xen acts as a conduit for the guest domains to communicate with the outside world. All network traffic sent to and received by the guest domains goes through and is forwarded by dom0. Routing uses the IP addresses to figure out where to send the network packets.

Routing acts at a higher level than the bridging technique, which only looked at the MAC address to find out the destination. Routing and bridging accomplish the same task, but use different methods to move information from source to destination. IP forwarding relays packets from one network segment to another if the proper routing entries exist in the routing table. In this case we are using unicast, which relays a packet from one link to another along a chain that connects the packet from source to destination.

When we utilized the bridging configuration in the earlier section, we used broadcasting, which duplicates a packet and sends a copy to each of the multiple links, thus delivering a copy to every device on the network. Essentially, routing buffers and forwards network data packets to their destination addresses. When we use routed networking, dom0 acts as a router to the outside world and a junction between the outside world and the guest domains, and buffers and transfers data packets among the domains. dom0 is the only domain that is actually connected to the physical Ethernet interface, and all the traffic from the various domains to the outside world go through it. It creates, maintains and uses a routing table in order to send the network packets to the right destinations.

The routed network configuration work on network packets while the bridged network configuration works on Ethernet frames. So, while a network bridge will direct the Ethernet frames by utilizing hardware MAC addresses, a network router will make routing decisions based on assigned IP Addresses. This enables network packets to be forwarded by the router from one host to another based on the addressing scheme, without the need to know or maintain the entire path from source to destination.

In this section we will look at what happens behind the scenes and how Xen actually sets up your network configuration to use routing.

Time for Action—Using Routed Networking

We are going to configure the domU to use routed networking, and then create a guest domain that uses routed networking.

1. We need to stop xend first as we will be modifying its configuration file:

   ```
   # service xend stop
   ```

2. Change the xen configuration file - `/etc/xen/xend-config.sxp` so we can use routed networking. Comment out the two lines related to the bridged networking and uncomment the two lines related to routed networking. If you don't happen to have the routed networking lines in your configuration file, add them:

   ```
   (network-script network-route)
   (vif-script     vif-route)
   ```

3. Start xend again so that it starts up with the new settings:

   # xend start

4. Modify the configuration file for the domU we used earlier so that it can use routed networking.

```
kernel = "/boot/vmlinuz-2.6.16.38-xenU"
memory = 32
name = "routed_domU"
disk = ['tap:aio:/home/pchaganti/xen-
       images/ttylinux_domU.img,hda,w']
vif = [ 'ip=192.168.1.165' ]
root = "/dev/hda1 ro"
```

5. Start up the domU.

   # xm create /home/pchaganti/xen-images/ttylinux_domU.cfg -c

6. Check to make sure the domU is up and running.

```
[root@gandalf xen-images]# xm list
Name                                      ID   Mem VCPUs      State   Time(s)
Domain-0                                   0   129     1     r-----   27144.4
routed-domU                                9    32     1     -b----       0.3
[root@gandalf xen-images]#
```

What Just Happened?

Here is the sequence of events that happens when xend starts up with a routed network configuration (only dom0 is started up in this instance. I have only one physical network interface on my server and it is named `eth0`);

1. Enable IP forwarding within dom0.
2. That is essentially all that xend does to get the network configured. Check the network configuration and list the interfaces created by running the `ifconfig` command.

```
[root@gandalf ~]# ifconfig
eth0      Link encap:Ethernet  HWaddr 00:13:D3:93:20:49
          inet addr:192.168.1.86  Bcast:192.168.1.255  Mask:255.255.255.0
          UP BROADCAST RUNNING MULTICAST  MTU:1500  Metric:1
          RX packets:21700 errors:0 dropped:0 overruns:0 frame:0
          TX packets:23509 errors:0 dropped:0 overruns:0 carrier:0
          collisions:745 txqueuelen:1000
          RX bytes:4397159 (4.1 MiB)  TX bytes:8305684 (7.9 MiB)
          Interrupt:16 Base address:0xdd00

lo        Link encap:Local Loopback
          inet addr:127.0.0.1  Mask:255.0.0.0
          UP LOOPBACK RUNNING  MTU:16436  Metric:1
          RX packets:40429 errors:0 dropped:0 overruns:0 frame:0
          TX packets:40429 errors:0 dropped:0 overruns:0 carrier:0
          collisions:0 txqueuelen:0
          RX bytes:8472608 (8.0 MiB)  TX bytes:8472608 (8.0 MiB)

[root@gandalf ~]#
```

3. Display the contents of the routing table used by the Xen server by running the `route` command. In our case, the contents of the routing table are as follows:

```
[root@gandalf ~]# route -n
Kernel IP routing table
Destination     Gateway         Genmask         Flags Metric Ref    Use Iface
192.168.1.0     0.0.0.0         255.255.255.0   U     0      0        0 eth0
169.254.0.0     0.0.0.0         255.255.0.0     U     0      0        0 eth0
0.0.0.0         192.168.1.254   0.0.0.0         UG    0      0        0 eth0
[root@gandalf ~]#
```

4. The following diagram shows the routed network configuration and the network interfaces created when only dom0 is running.

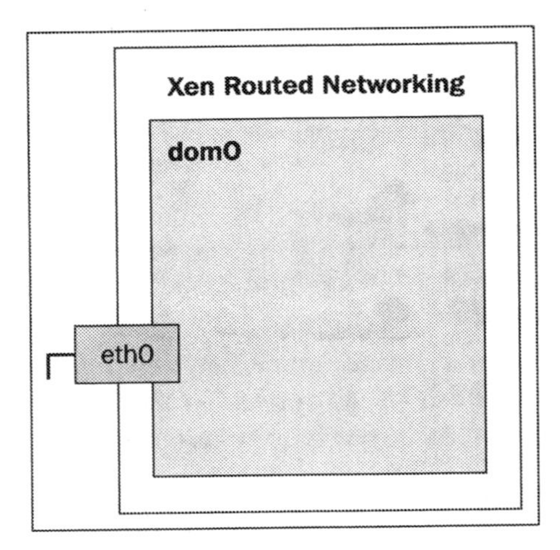

5. When the domU is started up, the following sequence of events takes place:
    - Xen copies the IP address from `eth0` to the virtual interface `vif<id#>.0`. The virtual interface ID is automatically assigned to each of the guest domain started up by Xen. The assigned id is never reused in a single session. So if you stop and restart a domain, a new ID will be assigned to it.
    - Brings up the virtual interface `vif<id#>.0`.
    - Adds a static route for the domU's IP address specified in domU configuration file that points to the virtual interface `vif<id#>.0`.

6. Here is the configuration of the network interfaces when both dom0 and domU are running.

```
[root@gandalf ~]# ifconfig
eth0      Link encap:Ethernet  HWaddr 00:13:D3:93:20:49
          inet addr:192.168.1.86  Bcast:192.168.1.255  Mask:255.255.255.0
          UP BROADCAST RUNNING MULTICAST  MTU:1500  Metric:1
          RX packets:22694 errors:0 dropped:0 overruns:0 frame:0
          TX packets:24688 errors:0 dropped:0 overruns:0 carrier:0
          collisions:935 txqueuelen:1000
          RX bytes:4482943 (4.2 MiB)  TX bytes:8783816 (8.3 MiB)
          Interrupt:16 Base address:0xdd00

lo        Link encap:Local Loopback
          inet addr:127.0.0.1  Mask:255.0.0.0
          UP LOOPBACK RUNNING  MTU:16436  Metric:1
          RX packets:42542 errors:0 dropped:0 overruns:0 frame:0
          TX packets:42542 errors:0 dropped:0 overruns:0 carrier:0
          collisions:0 txqueuelen:0
          RX bytes:8967204 (8.5 MiB)  TX bytes:8967204 (8.5 MiB)

vif5.0    Link encap:Ethernet  HWaddr FE:FF:FF:FF:FF:FF
          inet addr:192.168.1.86  Bcast:192.168.1.86  Mask:255.255.255.255
          UP BROADCAST RUNNING MULTICAST  MTU:1500  Metric:1
          RX packets:0 errors:0 dropped:0 overruns:0 frame:0
          TX packets:14 errors:0 dropped:0 overruns:0 carrier:0
          collisions:0 txqueuelen:32
          RX bytes:0 (0.0 b)  TX bytes:3495 (3.4 KiB)

[root@gandalf ~]#
```

7. The following screenshot shows the entries in the network routing table when domU is started up. You can now see an entry was added to it for routing packets to the virtual network interface for domU.

```
[root@gandalf ~]# route -n
Kernel IP routing table
Destination     Gateway         Genmask         Flags Metric Ref    Use Iface
192.168.1.155   0.0.0.0         255.255.255.255 UH    0      0        0 vif5.0
192.168.1.0     0.0.0.0         255.255.255.0   U     0      0        0 eth0
169.254.0.0     0.0.0.0         255.255.0.0     U     0      0        0 eth0
0.0.0.0         192.168.1.254   0.0.0.0         UG    0      0        0 eth0
[root@gandalf ~]#
```

8. The following diagram shows a complete Xen routed network configuration with a dom0 and one domU running.

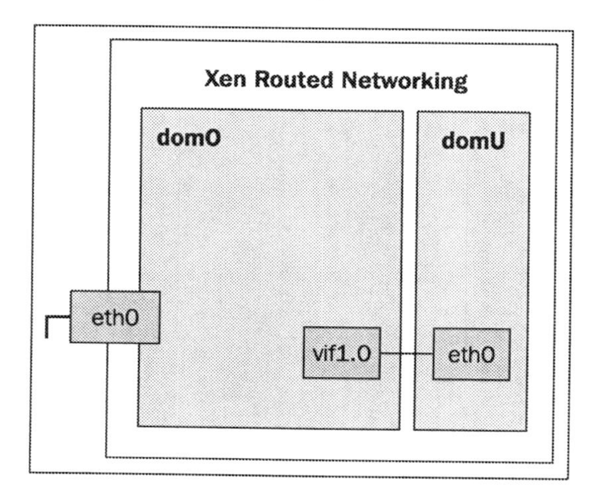

Virtual Local Network with Network Address Translation

In this section we are going to set up a Xen networking configuration that has a dom0 with a public IP address that acts as a router to a VLAN by using NAT. The VLAN can have any number of virtual machines, all of which will use a new network interface that is connected to the bridge. In the previous chapter each of our virtual machines had a separate public IP address assigned to it that made things easier. However in this section, we will use a single IP address and still provide the ability to connect to any port on a virtual machine on our VLAN by using address translation.

We will set up a VLAN with one webserver and one database. Each of these has a private IP address that is not available on the regular network. The only public IP address will be that of dom0. When a request comes in to dom0 with its IP address but a webserver port of 80, we will use NAT to forward the request to the webserver virtual machine inside the VLAN, and similarly when a request is made for the database port we will send it on to the database vm.

Time for Action—Using VLAN with NAT

We will create a virtual network with the IP address 192.168.2.0 with one webserver and a database. All the virtual machines in this network will have IP addresses in that range. We will create two virtual machines in this network and access them from a single public IP address. The ports will be forwarded to the respective virtual machines by dom0.

1. The first network interface is being used by dom0. We are going to create a new network interface that will be used by our VLAN. This interface will be created using a dummy network driver and named dummy0. Create a new file named `/etc/sysconfig/network-scripts/ifcfg-dummy0`:

```
A DEVICE=dummy0
BOOTPROTO=none
ONBOOT=yes
USERCTL=no
IPV6INIT=no
PEERDNS=yes
TYPE=Ethernet
NETMASK=255.255.255.0
IPADDR=x.x.x.x
ARP=yes
```

2. Assign an IP address to this interface and add it to the network interfaces file — `/etc/network/interfaces`:

```
auto dummy0
iface dummy0 inet static
       address 192.168.2.1
       netmask 255.255.255.0
```

3. Modify the xend configuration — `/etc/xen/xend-config.sxp` so that we can bind the bridge to the new dummy network interface dummy0 by adding the following line:

```
(network-script 'network-bridge netdev=dummy0')
```

4. Ensure that IP forwarding is enabled.

```
# echo "1" > /proc/sys/net/ipv4/ip_forward
```

5. Restart `sysctl` so that the changes are picked up by the live kernel.

```
# /sbin/sysctl -p
```

6. Create the first virtual machine on our VLAN. Use any of the guest domains that we have been using in this book. Modify its configuration file to look as follows:

```
# assume this is the webserver vm
kernel = "/boot/vmlinuz-2.6.16.38-xenU"
memory = 32
name = "vlan_domU_1"
disk = ['tap:aio:/home/pchaganti/xen-
        images/ttylinux_domU.img,hda,w']
vif = [ 'ip=192.168.2.2' ]
root = "/dev/hda1 ro"
gateway="192.168.2.1"
```

7. Create the second virtual machine on our VLAN. Use any of the guest domains used in this book. Modify its configuration file to look as follows:

```
# assume this is the mysql vm
kernel = "/boot/vmlinuz-2.6.16.38-xenU"
memory = 32
name = "vlan_domU_2"
disk = ['tap:aio:/home/pchaganti/xen-
        images/ttylinux_domU.img,hda,w']
vif = [ 'ip=192.168.2.3' ]
root = "/dev/hda1 ro"
gateway="192.168.2.1"
```

8. Inform dom0 that it should forward requests for certain ports to this VLAN. In order to do this, first we need to enable NAT on dom0:

```
# iptables -t nat -A POSTROUTING -s 192.168.0.0/16 -j MASQUERADE
```

9. We can now set up rules for forwarding the ports to the correct virtual machine. Let's first forward port 80:

```
# iptables -A PREROUTING -t nat -p tcp -i eth0 --dport 80 -j
     DNAT -- to 192.168.2.2:80
```

10. Forward the mysql port 3306 next:

```
# iptables -A PREROUTING -t nat -p tcp -i eth0 --dport 3306 -j
     DNAT --to 192.168.2.3:3306
```

Restart xend and create the virtual machines. Now we have a simple network configuration with the dom0 forwarding requests to a guest domain inside a VLAN based on the port. If the public IP address of dom0 is 10.10.1.176, making a request of 10.10.1.176:80, dom0 will send on the request to 192.168.2.2:80, inside the VLAN.

What Just Happened?

We leveraged a single available IP address and used the technique of NAT to forward requests to virtual machines inside a VLAN. This is a fairly powerful technique making it easy to add additional guest domains inside the network and provide access to them by forwarding requests from dom0. You can add domains anywhere on the physical network but they will appear as part of the same subnet.

Summary

In this chapter we explored three different ways of configuring networking when using Xen:

- **Bridged networking**: Connects two network segments by using a network bridge and utilizes the hardware MAC addresses.
- **Routed networking**: Dom0 becomes the central point that routes all of the traffic for the guest domains.
- **VLAN with Network Address Translation**: Dom0 uses NAT to send requests to a Virtual Local Network.

In the next chapter, we are going to examine the various storage options that are available when creating guest domains with Xen.

6
Storage

We need some kind of storage for saving the new virtual machines that we create. With Xen, there is an option to use a wide variety of storage solutions for the guest domains—from normal disk storage to logical volume managed storage and network storage. This chapter will show you how to use each of these storage technologies while creating new virtual machines. We will also discuss a few of the advanced storage options available for use with Xen.

- File storage
- Network File System (NFS) storage
- Logical Volume Managed (LVM) storage

Files

Simple files can be used as virtual block devices containing Xen domains. This is the quickest way to get started using Xen. We used them in Chapter 3 when we were setting up various operating systems to run as Xen guest domains. In Chapter 3 in the *Time for Action – Bootstrapping an Ubuntu system* we created the files that hold are guest domain and then installed Ubuntu on them.

We created the files for holding the guest domain and then installed Ubuntu to them in Chapter 3.

File-backed virtual block devices are a convenient way to get started with Xen. We use the venerable `dd` command to create the file that will be used to store our image. Doing this ensures that the file will be sparse, and space will be allocated only as parts of the file are used, not up front when the file is created.

Although files are a simple and quick way of storing VMs, there are some disadvantages of using files as virtual block devices:

- They are not suitable for I/O-intensive uses, as they experience some slowdown under heavy I/O workloads. The loopback block device used to support file-backed VBDs in dom0 performs the I/O handling quite poorly.
- Linux by default, supports a maximum of eight file-backed VBDs across all domains. This limit can, however, be increased by utilizing the `max_loop` kernel parameter if the `CONFIG_BLK_DEV_LOOP` command is compiled as a module in the dom0 kernel.

NFS

Network File System (NFS) is a client/server system that enables users to access files across a network and treat them as though they are in a local file directory. An NFS server provides remote clients with access to its files by exporting the files that are mounted by the remote client and made available to the operating system and the user.

NFS is a great way to allow a system to share directories and files with other systems over a network. It enables users to access files on remote systems almost as though they were local files. Some of the advantages of NFS are as follows:

- Disk space usage on local machines is reduced considerably by storing most of the commonly used and accessed data on a single machine accessible to others over the network.
- Home directories for individual users on a system could be set up and stored on a remote NFS server and made available throughout the network.
- Storage devices can be set up on a remote NFS server. Furthermore, access provided to the devices through NFS exports reduces the enterprise hardware requirements.
- Remote boot linux machines via a NFS root file system across the network.

Xen enables us to utilize the power of NFS by booting guest domains with a root file system that is available through NFS. In this section we will examine how we can boot a guest Xen domain that uses an exported NFS file system as its root file system.

Time for Action—Using NFS

In order to use NFS, we will first need a Xen domU kernel with NFS support.

1. Most kernels will support NFS out of the box, but in case yours does not, you need to compile the kernel with NFS support. Run the linux kernel configuration for the domU kernel.

```
# make linux-2.6-xenU-config CONFIGMODE=menuconfig
```

2. Select the **File systems** option:

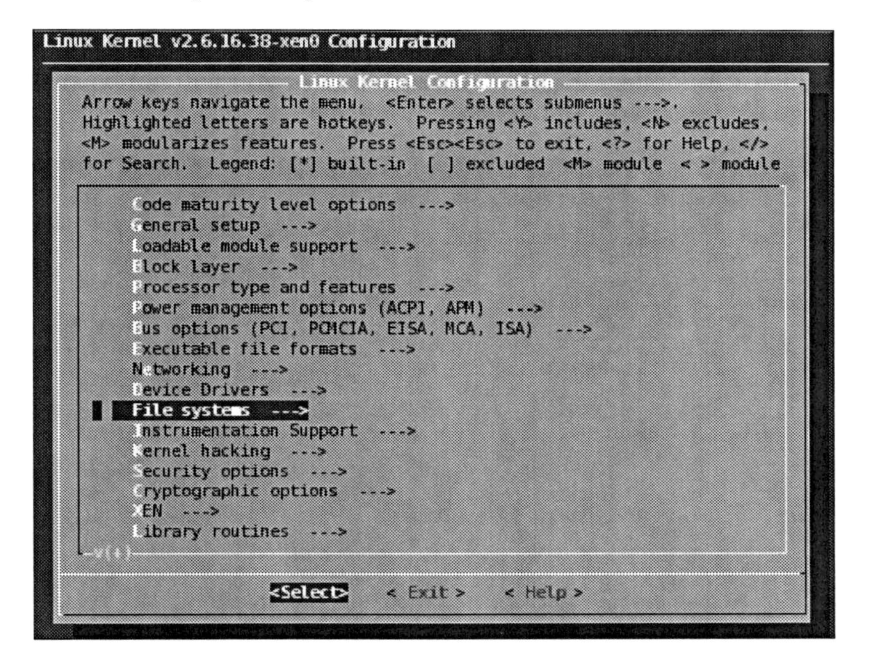

3. Select **Network File systems**:

```
Linux Kernel v2.6.16.38-xen0 Configuration
                         File systems
Arrow keys navigate the menu.  <Enter> selects submenus --->.
Highlighted letters are hotkeys.  Pressing <Y> includes, <N> excludes,
<M> modularizes features.  Press <Esc><Esc> to exit, <?> for Help, </>
for Search.  Legend: [*] built-in  [ ] excluded  <M> module  < > module
  < > Reiserfs support
  < > JFS filesystem support
  < > XFS filesystem support
  < > OCFS2 file system support (EXPERIMENTAL)
  < > Minix fs support
  < > ROM file system support
  [*] Inotify file change notification support
  [ ] Quota support
  <*> Kernel automounter support
  <*> Kernel automounter version 4 support (also supports v3)
  < > Filesystem in Userspace support
      CD-ROM/DVD Filesystems  --->
      DOS/FAT/NT Filesystems  --->
      Pseudo filesystems  --->
      Miscellaneous filesystems  --->
      Network File Systems  --->
      Partition Types  --->

            <Select>    < Exit >    < Help >
```

4. Select the options—**NFS File system support** and **Root file system on NFS**. Select them to be compiled in the kernel. You can also choose to turn them into modules if you like. If you do turn them into modules, please make sure that you include them in your `initrd` image or you will not be able to boot your guest domain off an NFS root file system.

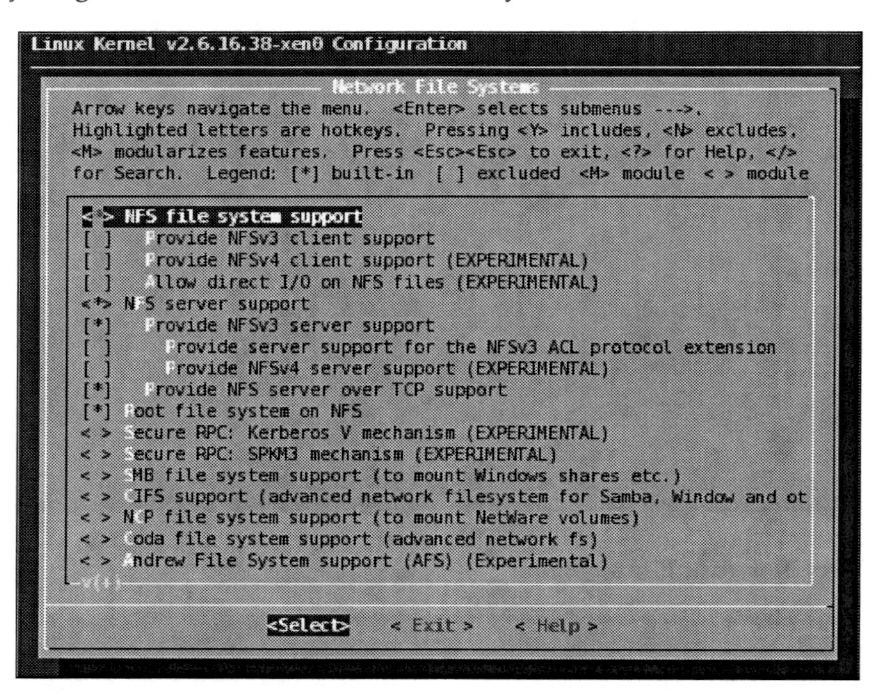

5. Compile the kernel and install it:

```
make linux-2.6-xen0-build
make linux-2.6-xen0-install
```

6. Reboot to pick up your new changes:

7. We now need a NFS server we can use. You can use an existing one if you have access to one. We will set up a new NFS server for this section on a new server (IP 192.168.1.67). This server is running Ubuntu Feisty Fawn, and some of the commands for installing packages will be specific to Debian. Replace them with your distribution-specific package management commands:

8. Install the NFS server and portmap packges. The portmap and NFS server daemons will be started automatically after the installation. Double check to make sure that your distribution does the same:

```
# apt-get install nfs-user-server portmap
```

9. Create a directory that will contain our guest installation. This will be the directory that we export from this server via NFS:

```
# mkdir /mnt/feisty
```

10. Add this directory to the directories that are exported by editing the `/etc/exports` file:

```
# /mnt/feisty        192.168.1.86(rw,sync,no_root_squash)
```

11. Populate this directory with Ubuntu Feisty by using *debootstrap*. This will download and extract all the necessary files to the above mounted directory:

```
~ /usr/sbin/debootstrap --arch i386 feisty /mnt/feisty
            http://archive.ubuntu.com/ubuntu
```

12. We will be using the domU kernel modules from our Xen server system. Copy them from the /lib/modules directory to this directory:

```
scp -r pchaganti@192.168.1.86:/lib/modules/2.6.16.38-xenU
                /mnt/feisty/lib/modules/
```

13. Now `chroot` into this new system and configure it:

```
~ chroot /mnt/feisty /bin/bash
```

14. Add the packages that we will need:

```
# apt-get install nfs-common portmap
```

15. Set the hostname for this system:

```
~ echo "ubuntu_feisty_nfs_domU" > /etc/hostname
```

16. Set up the filesystems that will be loaded on boot:

```
cat > /etc/fstab << "EOF"
# file system    mount point   type    options      dump pass
192.168.1.67:/mnt/feisty         nfs     rw          0    0
proc             /proc         proc    defaults      0    0
sys              /sys          sysfs   defaults      0    0
EOF
```

17. Set up the network. We will be using the loopback interface and eth0 for the Ethernet connection. The `eth0` interface will be using DHCP to set itself up automatically:

```
cat > /etc/network/interfaces << "EOF"
# The loopback network interface
auto lo
iface lo inet loopback

# The primary network interface
auto eth0
iface eth0 inet dhcp

EOF
```

18. Add a user, create an admin group, put the added user in to this group, and set the root password:

    ```
    # adduser pchaganti
    # addgroup --system admin
    # adduser pchaganti admin
    # passwd root
    ```

19. Ubuntu uses `sudo` to let users perform administrative functions. Use `visudo` to edit the `sudoers` file:

    ```
    visudo
    # Members of the admin group may gain root privileges
    %admin ALL=(ALL) ALL
    ```

20. Create the xen config file for this domU:

    ```
    cat > /home/pchaganti/xen-images/ubuntu_feisty_nfs_domU.cfg <<
         "EOF"
    kernel = "/boot/vmlinuz-2.6.16.38-xenU"
    memory = 256
    name = "ubuntu_feisty_nfs_domU"
    vif = [ 'ip=192.168.1.111' ]
    nfs_server = '192.168.1.67'
    nfs_root   = '/mnt/feisty'
    root       = '/dev/nfs'
    EOF
    ```

21. Start up the Ubuntu Feisty domain using `xm`:

    ```
    # xm create ubuntu_feisty_nfs_domU.cfg -c
    ```

What Just Happened?

In this section we set up a directory to be exported via NFS from a remote server. We then installed Ubuntu Feisty Fawn into this directory using *debootstrap*. The configuration file for the domain specified the various parameters necessary for Xen to recognize that the guest domain will be using NFS for boot up. This enables you to consolidate some of your storage requirements. However, keep in mind the following when using NFS:

- The restrictions on the exported directories must be set very carefully to ensure that access is only provided to the right servers.
- NFS is quite fast, but it still has to deal with the overhead of creating and closing network connections and transferring data over the network. If speed is of paramount importance to your Xen domains, NFS is not the way to go.

- There are a couple of different versions of NFS—NFS v3 and NFS v4. You will need to examine their features carefully to determine which one will be a better fit for your needs.

The following links provide more information on NFS:

- NFS how to: `http://nfs.sourceforge.net/nfs-howto/`
- Understanding NFS: `http://www.onlamp.com/lpt/a/1548`

Logical Volume Management

LVM is a partitioning scheme designed to be more flexible than normal physical disk partitioning. It allows changes in the size of individual volumes without a reboot, and, in most cases, while the file system on the volume is being actively used. It is the recommended way to deploy Xen domains in production. LVM can create "virtual" disk partitions out of one or more physical hard drives and makes it possible to dynamically group them into a virtual single chunk of storage. You can grow, shrink, or move those partitions from drive to drive. You can even create larger partitions than you could with a single drive.

The main components of LVM are as follows:

- **Physical volume**: These are the hard disks or disk partitions that are visible to the operating system. Each physical volume is in turn split up into smaller chunks called *physical extents* (PEs).
- **Volume group**: A volume group is an abstraction representing a collection of physical volumes from which logical volumes can be created, thus combines the two into one easy to administer unit of storage.
- **Logical volume**: A logical volume is a virtual device and represents an addressable consecutive space of block storage.
- **Physical extent**: Each physical volume is divided into physical extents, each of which is the same size as the logical extents for the volume group.
- **Logical extent**: Each logical volume is split into logical extents.

Some of the main advantages of using LVM are as follows:

- Ability to resize the volume groups.
- Ability to resize logical volumes without taking down the server.
- Ability to create read-only snapshots of logical volumes.
- Ability to move logical volumes between physical volumes.
- Ability to split or merge volume groups. This is used for migrating logical volumes to or from offline storage.

In this section we will create a Ubuntu Feisty Fawn installation on LVM volume.

Time for Action—Using LVM

We will create the volumes needed for our installation first, and then install Ubuntu onto the volume.

1. Create a physical volume on a disk partition:

   ```
   # pvcreate /dev/hda6
   ```

2. Display the details of the various physical volumes present in your system:

```
[root@gandalf ~]# pvdisplay
  --- Physical volume ---
  PV Name               /dev/hda6
  VG Name               gandalf
  PV Size               62.85 GB / not usable 11.33 MB
  Allocatable           yes
  PE Size (KByte)       32768
  Total PE              2011
  Free PE               1230
  Allocated PE          781
  PV UUID               xzu0gz-2c13-i3xz-hS3T-FQs0-xHzY-pATMBR

[root@gandalf ~]#
```

3. Create a volume group on the physical volume with a name `gandalf`:

   ```
   # vgcreate gandalf /dev/hda6
   ```

4. You can display the various volume groups present on your server by using the `vgdisplay` command.

```
[root@gandalf ~]# vgdisplay
  --- Volume group ---
  VG Name               gandalf
  System ID
  Format                lvm2
  Metadata Areas        1
  Metadata Sequence No  2
  VG Access             read/write
  VG Status             resizable
  MAX LV                0
  Cur LV                1
  Open LV               1
  Max PV                0
  Cur PV                1
  Act PV                1
  VG Size               62.84 GB
  PE Size               32.00 MB
  Total PE              2011
  Alloc PE / Size       781 / 24.41 GB
  Free  PE / Size       1230 / 38.44 GB
  VG UUID               ktGy21-4oKo-n6BU-tOLG-HMtJ-RFjH-Z1CodE

[root@gandalf ~]#
```

5. Create a logical volume for storing our image and name the volume `feisty`:

   # lvcreate -L 4094M -n feisty gandalf

6. The logical volume details can de displayed by using the `lvdisplay` command.

```
[root@gandalf ~]# lvdisplay
  --- Logical volume ---
  LV Name                /dev/gandalf/xen
  VG Name                gandalf
  LV UUID                Brv2jQ-r50c-oJHo-sUX3-P6o5-GP6N-4l2taN
  LV Write Access        read/write
  LV Status              available
  # open                 1
  LV Size                24.41 GB
  Current LE             781
  Segments               1
  Allocation             inherit
  Read ahead sectors     0
  Block device           254:0

  --- Logical volume ---
  LV Name                /dev/gandalf/feisty
  VG Name                gandalf
  LV UUID                NUsQ7U-zwFv-2BRc-c2y9-0fBv-90ii-3dR7Iy
  LV Write Access        read/write
  LV Status              available
  # open                 0
  LV Size                4.00 GB
  Current LE             128
  Segments               1
  Allocation             inherit
  Read ahead sectors     0
  Block device           254:1

[root@gandalf ~]#
```

7. The `lvscan` command is used to scan all the logical volumes and their current status. As you can see below, we have two logical volumes and both are currently active.

```
[root@gandalf ~]# lvscan
  ACTIVE            '/dev/gandalf/xen' [24.41 GB] inherit
  ACTIVE            '/dev/gandalf/feisty' [4.00 GB] inherit
[root@gandalf ~]#
```

8. Create the ext3 file system on our newly created logical volume.

```
[root@gandalf ~]# mkfs.ext3 /dev/gandalf/feisty
mke2fs 1.39 (29-May-2006)
Filesystem label=
OS type: Linux
Block size=4096 (log=2)
Fragment size=4096 (log=2)
524288 inodes, 1048576 blocks
52428 blocks (5.00%) reserved for the super user
First data block=0
Maximum filesystem blocks=1073741824
32 block groups
32768 blocks per group, 32768 fragments per group
16384 inodes per group
Superblock backups stored on blocks:
        32768, 98304, 163840, 229376, 294912, 819200, 884736

Writing inode tables: done
Creating journal (32768 blocks): done
Writing superblocks and filesystem accounting information: done

This filesystem will be automatically checked every 21 mounts or
180 days, whichever comes first.  Use tune2fs -c or -i to override.
[root@gandalf ~]#
```

9. Create a directory and mount the logical volume:

```
# mkdir /mnt/feisty
# mount /dev/gandalf/feisty /mnt/feisty
```

10. Run *debootstrap*. This will download and extract all the necessary files to the above mounted directory:

```
~ /usr/sbin/debootstrap --arch i386 feisty /mnt/feisty
    http://archive.ubuntu.com/ubuntu
```

11. We will be using the domU kernel that we created earlier for booting this domain. So this domain will need the kernel modules compiled for that kernel. Copy them from the `/lib/modules` directory:

```
~ cp -dpR /lib/modules/2.6.16.38-xenU /mnt/feisty/lib/modules
```

12. Now `chroot` into this new system and configure it:

```
~ chroot /mnt/feisty /bin/sh
```

13. Set the hostname for this system:

```
~ echo "ubuntu_feisty_domU" > /etc/hostname
```

14. Set up the filesystems that will be loaded on boot:

```
cat > /etc/fstab << "EOF"
# file system    mount point    type     options     dump  pass
/dev/sda1        /              ext3     defaults     0     1
proc             /proc          proc     defaults     0     0
sys              /sys           sysfs    defaults     0     0
EOF
```

15. Setup the network. We will be using the loopback interface and eth0 for the ethernet connection. The `eth0` interface will be using DHCP to set itself up automatically:

```
cat > /etc/network/interfaces << "EOF"
# The loopback network interface
auto lo
iface lo inet loopback
# The primary network interface
auto eth0
iface eth0 inet dhcp
EOF
```

16. Add a user, create an admin group, put the added user in this group, and set the root password:

```
# adduser pchaganti
# addgroup --system admin
# adduser pchaganti admin
# passwd root
```

17. Ubuntu uses `sudo` to let users perform administrative functions. Use `visudo` to edit the `sudoers` file:

```
visudo
# Members of the admin group may gain root privileges
%admin ALL=(ALL) ALL
```

18. We have completed the initial configuration. Exit out of the `chroot` environment:

```
# exit
# umount /mnt/feisty
```

19. Create the configuration file that will be used by dom0 to create this guest domain:

```
cat > /home/pchaganti/xen-images/ubuntu_feisty_domU.cfg << "EOF"
kernel = "/boot/vmlinuz-2.6.16.38-xenU"
memory = 256
name = "ubuntu_feisty_domU"
disk = ['phy:gandalf/feisty']
vif = [ 'mac=00:16:3e:00:00:10, bridge=xenbr0' ]
root = "/dev/sda1 ro"
EOF
```

20. Call `xm` to create the virtual machine:

```
# xm create /home/pchaganti/xen-images/ubuntu_feisty_domU .cfg -c
```

What Just Happened?

In this section we created a new logical volume named *feisty* and populated it with Ubuntu feisty using the *debootstrap* tool. We exported this logical volume to Xen by referencing it as a physical device.

The use of LVM storage for Xen domains is encouraged, as it is probably the ideal way to set up and administer the domains. However, please note that using LVM in guests with LVM on the host can cause problems as the inside guests can see the wrong LVM information from the host. However, LVM makes it extremely easy to manage storage requirements for the enterprise while providing a configurable and adaptable virtualization environment. Here are some links that provide more detailed information on LVM:

- LVM How to: `http://www.tldp.org/HOWTO/html_single/LVM-HOWTO/`
- Learning Linux LVM: `http://www.ibm.com/developerworks/linux/library/l-lvm/`
- Managing disk space with LVM: `http://www.linuxdevcenter.com/lpt/a/6553`

Advanced Storage Options

Some advanced storage options such as Redundant Array of Independent/Inexpensive Drives (RAID) and Global Network Block Device (GNBD) are discussed in this section.

Redundant Array of Independent/Inexpensive Drives

RAID is a data storage scheme for dividing and replicating data among multiple hard disk drives. It spreads data among several physical hard drives with enough redundancy so that should any drive fail, the data will still be intact. Once created, a RAID array is a device that can be used pretty much like a regular partition. It provides increased data reliability and greatly improved input and output performances.

The three key concepts in RAID are as follows:

- **Mirroring**: Copying the data to more than one disk.
- **Striping**: Splitting the data across more than one disk and reading sequences of data simultaneously off multiple disks.
- **Fault tolerance**: Increasing the reliability of the system by storing some redundant data, so that problems can be detected and possibly fixed quickly.

The biggest advantage of using RAID is that systems can be designed to keep working when there is failure—hot swapping of disks and automatic data recovery even while the system keeps running. For this reason RAID is often used in high availability systems, where it is critical that the system keeps running for as much of the time as possible. The following resources will help you to get Xen working using RAID storage:

- Setting up Xen with LVM and RAID:
  `http://www.webhostingtalk.com/archive/index.php/t-563457.html`
- LVM on a RAID mirror for Xen:
  `http://www.jukie.net/~bart/blog/20060410220525`

Global Network Block Device

GNBD provides storage access over an Ethernet LAN, thus allowing you to share and access logical block devices across the network. We have done something similar earlier in this chapter using NFS. A common usage scenario of GNBD is to export the logical block devices from LVM. It is a simple and inexpensive substitute for a Storage Area Network (SAN) like configuration. Please be aware that one potential drawback with using a GNBD is a possible reduction in the speed of your network. Unless you have a blazing fast network, its speed will not be as fast as the speed of reading from a disk.

The following resources could be useful for setting up GNBD:

- How to build, install, and run GNBD:
  `http://sources.redhat.com/cluster/gnbd/gnbd_usage.txt`
- Xen with DRBD, GNBD and OCFS2 Howto:
  `http://xenamo.sourceforge.net/`

Summary

In this chapter we explored three different storage mechanisms that can be utilized for the guest domains:

- **Files**: These are simple file based virtual block devices that are very easy to get started with. They are great for testing, but are not recommended for production environments.
- **NFS**: These are remote file systems that can be exported and used by the Xen to boot guest domains. These require the setup of a remote NFS server that can export a file system. They are perform well and are widely used for setting up Xen domains.

- **LVM**: This is an enterprise grade storage mechanism that makes it very easy to resize, move, and reconfigure the storage to adapt to the changing needs of an enterprise, and is probably the most recommended production configuration for a Xen deployment.

We also discussed some advanced storage options that are available for use with Xen. In the next chapter, we will examine some options for encrypting root file systems for guest domains when using Xen.

7
Encryption

In this chapter we will secure guest domains by encrypting their root file system. Security in Xen is very important as improvements are being made to it all the time. Encrypting the root file system for a domain provides an extra layer of security over and above restricting physical access to the domain. You can encrypt not only the partitions that contain the root file system, but also those which are used by the domains. An encrypted file system prevents any information from being available to a malicious user who gains physical access to the system while it is not running. The files and the data in them will appear garbled and will be practically useless. The algorithms used provide a strong encryption of the file system data.

The key thing to be aware of here is that hackers could access information if they gain physical access to the system while it is running and the files in use are in a decrypted form. So it is very important to have controls in place to restrict physical access to the systems appropriately. However, file system encryption will keep any unauthorized person from booting up the system.

We will use the following methods of file system encryption:

- Plain device mapper-based encryption.
- Key based-device mapper encryption using LUKS.

Device Mapper-Based Encryption

A device mapper enables the definition of new partitions or logical volumes by specifying ranges of sectors on existing block devices. The ranges specified are then mapped to targets according to a mapping table. *dm-crypt* is a package that provides a target that can be used to transparently encrypt block devices using the kernel `cryptoAPI`. This is available only in the Linux 2.6 kernel series. The older kernels used *cryptoloop* to provide similar support, but that package has been deprecated. In this section we will learn how to use a simple device mapper-based encryption using the *dm-crypt* package.

Time for Action—Encrypting Block Devices

We will first prepare our kernel with all the needed modules and options to support the encryption. Then we will create the file backed virtual block device that will hold our guest domain and install Ubuntu to it.

1. Select the kernel options for the **Device Drivers**.

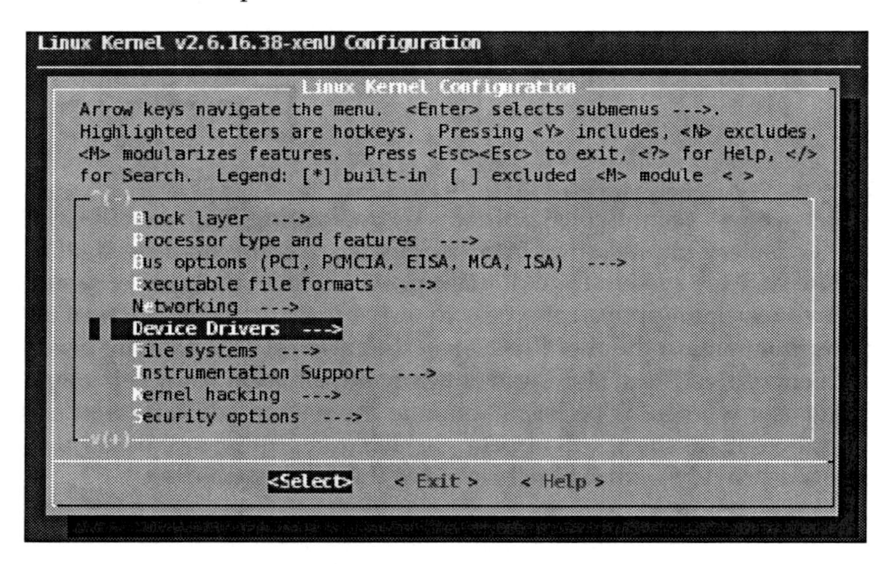

2. Select the **Multi-device support (RAID and LVM)** option.

```
Linux Kernel v2.6.16.38-xenU Configuration

                         Device Drivers
 Arrow keys navigate the menu.  <Enter> selects submenus --->.
 Highlighted letters are hotkeys.  Pressing <Y> includes, <N> excludes,
 <M> modularizes features.  Press <Esc><Esc> to exit, <?> for Help, </>
 for Search.  Legend: [*] built-in  [ ] excluded  <M> module  < >

     Memory Technology Devices (MTD)  --->
     Parallel port support  --->
     Plug and Play support  --->
     Block devices  --->
     ATA/ATAPI/MFM/RLL support  --->
     SCSI device support  --->
     Multi-device support (RAID and LVM)  --->
     Fusion MPT device support  --->
     IEEE 1394 (FireWire) support  --->
     I2O device support  --->

               <Select>    < Exit >    < Help >
```

3. Select the options—**Device mapper support and Crypt target support**. Select them to be compiled in to the kernel. You can also choose to make them modules. If you do so, please make sure that you have them included in your `initrd` image.

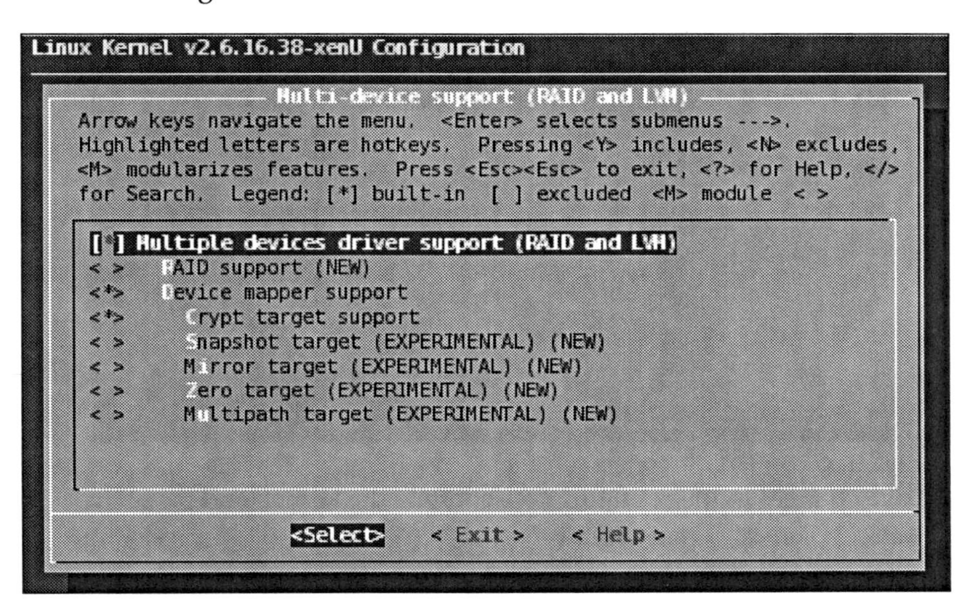

4. Select the **Cryptographic options** node in the kernel configuration:

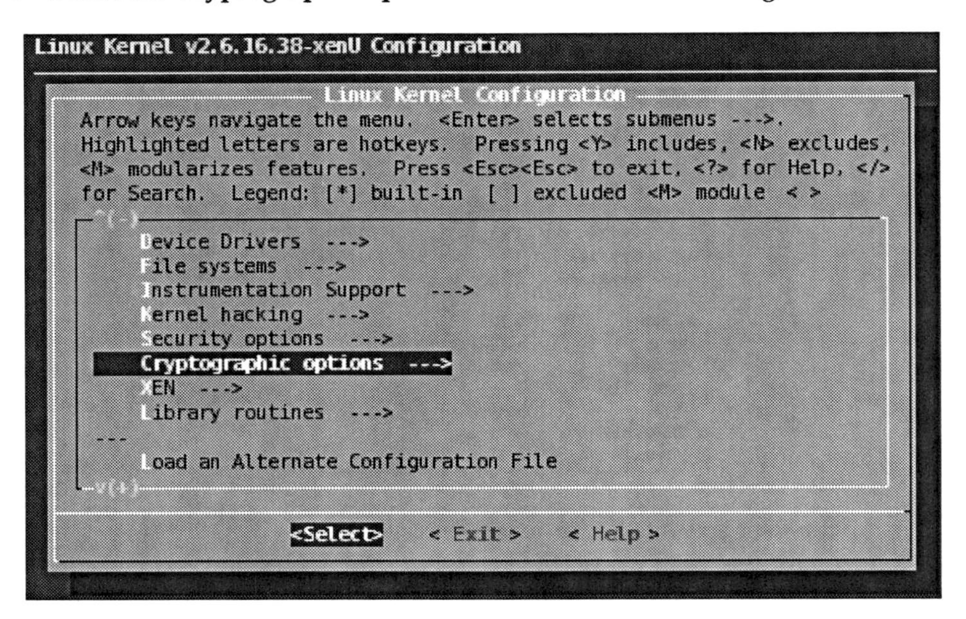

5. Select the **AES cipher algorithms** option. These algorithms are used for encryption by *dm-crypt*:

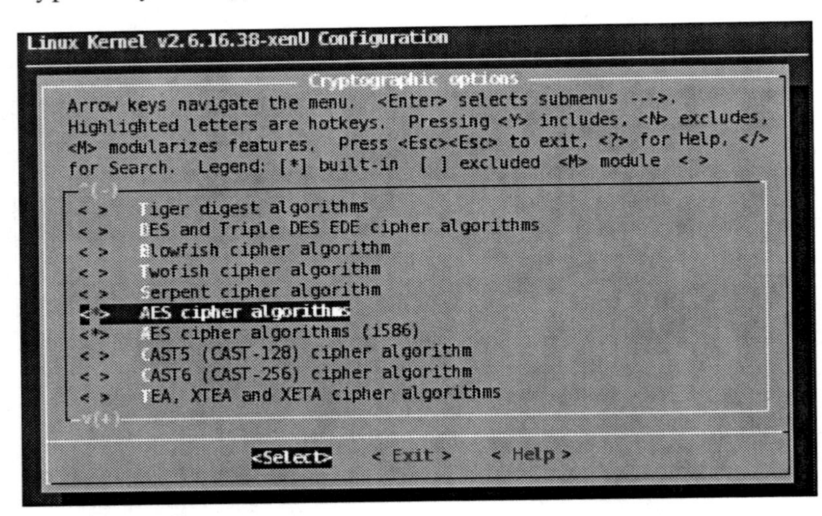

6. Save changes to the configuration, compile the kernel, and install it:

```
make linux-2.6-xen0-build
make linux-2.6-xen0-install
```

7. Reboot to pick up the new changes.

8. Check to make sure that you have support for AES:

```
# cat /proc/crypto
```

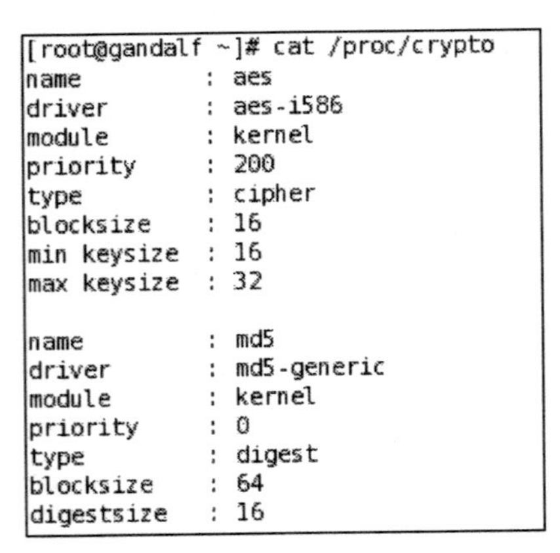

9. Install the user space tools for using *dm-crypt*:

```
# apt-get install cryptsetup dmsetup
```

10. We can display the names of the currently available targets by using `dmsetup`:
    `# dmsetup targets`

```
[root@gandalf ~]# dmsetup targets
mirror           v1.0.1
snapshot-origin  v1.4.0
snapshot         v1.4.0
crypt            v1.1.0
striped          v1.0.2
linear           v1.0.1
error            v1.0.1
[root@gandalf ~]#
```

11. We will use a loopback file to store our encrypted file system. Create a file that will contain the root file system for an Ubuntu Feisty installation:

```
# dd if=/dev/urandom of=/home/pchaganti/xen-images/
        ubuntu_feisty_domU.img bs=1G count=6
```

12. Set the loopback file created above as a loop device:

```
# losetup -f /home/pchaganti/xen-images/ubuntu_feisty_domU.img
```

13. Create a logical volume using the loop device. This will ask you for a passphrase. From this point on, whenever you mount this encrypted file, you will need to provide the passphrase:

```
# cryptsetup -y create encrypted_feisty /dev/loop0
```

14. Check to make sure that the volume was created correctly by using `dmsetup`:

```
# dmsetup ls
```

```
[root@gandalf xen-images]# dmsetup ls
gandalf-xen     (254, 0)
gandalf-feisty  (254, 1)
encrypted_feisty        (254, 2)
[root@gandalf xen-images]#
```

15. Create an ext3 file system on the encrypted file:

    ```
    # mkfs.ext3 /dev/mapper/encrypted_feisty
    ```

```
[root@gandalf xen-images]# mkfs.ext3 /dev/mapper/encrypted_feisty
mke2fs 1.39 (29-May-2006)
Filesystem label=
OS type: Linux
Block size=4096 (log=2)
Fragment size=4096 (log=2)
768544 inodes, 1536000 blocks
76800 blocks (5.00%) reserved for the super user
First data block=0
Maximum filesystem blocks=1572864000
47 block groups
32768 blocks per group, 32768 fragments per group
16352 inodes per group
Superblock backups stored on blocks:
        32768, 98304, 163840, 229376, 294912, 819200, 884736

Writing inode tables: done
Creating journal (32768 blocks): done
Writing superblocks and filesystem accounting information: done

This filesystem will be automatically checked every 39 mounts or
180 days, whichever comes first.  Use tune2fs -c or -i to override.
[root@gandalf xen-images]# 
```

16. Mount the encrypted file system:

    ```
    # mount /dev/mapper/encrypted_feisty /mnt/feisty
    ```

17. Now you can install Ubuntu into this mounted file system by following the steps that we have used earlier in this book. After you complete installing Ubuntu, unmount the file system.

18. Add the definition of the encrypted filesystem to `/etc/crypttab` directory:

    ```
    encrypted_feisty /dev/mapper/encrypted_feisty  none
                     check=ext3,retry=5
    ```

19. Add the device to the file systems that are mounted upon boot in `/etc/fstab`:

    ```
    /dev/mapper/encrypted-feisty /mnt/feisty  ext3 defaults 0 2
    ```

20. When you reboot, you will be asked for the passphrase before the file system can be mounted. Provide the passphrase and the file system will be mounted. Now you can start up your Ubuntu guest domain using a domain configuration file.

What Just Happened?

The device mapper provides a mechanism to create VBDs based on real block devices. We can put the VBDs through other things before letting the operating system access it. In case of using *dm-crypt*, we route it through the cryptographic API provided by the linux kernel, and apply high-level encryption to everything written to our filesystem.

Device Mapper-Based Encryption Using LUKS

Linux Unified Key Setup (LUKS) provides a standard format for encrypted partitions and enables multiple users/passwords. It also provides effective password revocation and security against low entropy attacks. In this section we will once again use a device mapper-based encryption scheme, but enhance it using LUKS.

Time for Action—by Extending dm-crypt

Since we will be using a device mapper-based encyption scheme as in the previous section, a lot of our initial steps will be same as the previous section, the main difference being that we will use the LUKS format for the hard disk encryption.

1. As described previously, ensure that you compile your kernel to have all the required modules. Also install the *dmsetup* and *cryptsetup* packages. In order to use LUKS, the kernel will need to support *SHA-256* algorithm. Select this option and compile it as a module or include it in the kernel. You can either insert the module into the running kernel or reboot if you include it in, to get the changes.

```
Linux Kernel v2.6.16.38-xen0 Configuration
 Cryptographic options
  Arrow keys navigate the menu.  <Enter> selects submenus --->.
  Highlighted letters are hotkeys.  Pressing <Y> includes, <N> excludes,
  <M> modularizes features.  Press <Esc><Esc> to exit, <?> for Help, </>
  for Search.  Legend: [*] built-in  [ ] excluded  <M> module  < >

   --- Cryptographic API
   [*]   HMAC support
   < >   Null algorithms
   < >   MD4 digest algorithm
   <*>   MD5 digest algorithm
   <*>   SHA1 digest algorithm
   < >   SHA256 digest algorithm
   < >   SHA384 and SHA512 digest algorithms
   < >   Whirlpool digest algorithms
   < >   Tiger digest algorithms
   v(+)

        <Select>    < Exit >    < Help >
```

2. We will once again use a loopback file to store our encrypted file system. Create a file that will contain the root file system for an Ubuntu Feisty installation:

```
# dd if=/dev/urandom of=/home/pchaganti/xen-images/
         ubuntu_feisty_domU.img bs=1G count=6
```

3. Set the loopback file created above as a loop device:

```
# losetup -f /home/pchaganti/xen-images/ubuntu_feisty_domU.img
```

4. Create a logical volume using the loop device. This will ask you for a passphrase. From this point on, whenever you mount this encrypted file, you will need to provide the passphrase:

```
# cryptsetup luksFormat /dev/loop0
```

```
[root@gandalf ~]# cryptsetup luksFormat /dev/loop0

WARNING!
========
This will overwrite data on /dev/loop0 irrevocably.

Are you sure? (Type uppercase yes): YES
Enter LUKS passphrase:
Verify passphrase:
Command successful.
[root@gandalf ~]#
```

5. Now create a device mapper for the loopback device:

```
# cryptsetup luksOpen /dev/loop0 encrypted_feisty_luks
```

```
[root@gandalf ~]# cryptsetup luksOpen /dev/loop0 encrypted_feisty_luks
Enter LUKS passphrase:
key slot 0 unlocked.
Command successful.
[root@gandalf ~]#
```

6. Create an ext3 file system on the encrypted file:

```
# mkfs.ext3 /dev/mapper/encrypted_feisty_luks
```

```
[root@gandalf ~]# mkfs.ext3 /dev/mapper/encrypted_feisty_luks
mke2fs 1.39 (29-May-2006)
Filesystem label=
OS type: Linux
Block size=4096 (log=2)
Fragment size=4096 (log=2)
768544 inodes, 1535871 blocks
76793 blocks (5.00%) reserved for the super user
First data block=0
Maximum filesystem blocks=1572864000
47 block groups
32768 blocks per group, 32768 fragments per group
16352 inodes per group
Superblock backups stored on blocks:
        32768, 98304, 163840, 229376, 294912, 819200, 884736

Writing inode tables: done
Creating journal (32768 blocks): done
Writing superblocks and filesystem accounting information: done

This filesystem will be automatically checked every 33 mounts or
180 days, whichever comes first.  Use tune2fs -c or -i to override.
[root@gandalf ~]#
```

7. Mount the new virtual device:

```
# mount /dev/mapper/Ubuntu_feisty_luks /mnt/feisty_luks
```

8. We have assigned one password for accessing this encrypted file system. LUKS provides support allowing you to add up to eight different passwords for access to this file system. This support enables you to provide multiple users with access. You can add new passwords by using the `luksAddKey` option:

```
# cryptsetup luksAddKey /dev/loop0
```

```
[root@gandalf ~]# cryptsetup luksAddKey /dev/loop0
Enter any LUKS passphrase:
Verify passphrase:
key slot 0 unlocked.
Enter new passphrase for key slot:
Verify passphrase:
Command successful.
[root@gandalf ~]#
```

9. You can get status information from the LUKS header. This will show you the open slots, the encryption algorithm used and other status information:

   # cryptsetup luksDump /dev/loop0

```
[root@gandalf ~]# cryptsetup luksDump /dev/loop0
LUKS header information for /dev/loop0

Version:        1
Cipher name:    aes
Cipher mode:    cbc-essiv:sha256
Hash spec:      sha1
Payload offset: 1032
MK bits:        128
MK digest:      8c 5f f2 9d aa 8e 97 95 b8 7f 34 4a f8 1a 26 56 f0 be e5 4c
MK salt:        18 73 51 9f 1e 85 a9 54 bf a5 1d 22 73 ed ac 08
                bb a1 88 97 ac 51 56 65 4e 07 81 b7 f1 2d 27 ab
MK iterations:  10
UUID:           f19e4258-1225-49a3-b228-6ba4cca3d04b

Key Slot 0: ENABLED
        Iterations:             159506
        Salt:                   43 20 a2 35 99 17 29 5f 7b d9 65 3b 21 6b 21 e4
                                d7 0b f4 39 4a 40 d6 66 8d 88 95 5c b4 47 47 22
        Key material offset:    8
        AF stripes:             4000
Key Slot 1: ENABLED
        Iterations:             159656
        Salt:                   0c fe 2f 38 7b 17 13 e0 68 e8 e4 d8 45 ab 7f 89
                                19 84 83 4f 59 5b 0c d3 d4 04 20 2a 30 53 9b a8
        Key material offset:    136
        AF stripes:             4000
Key Slot 2: DISABLED
Key Slot 3: DISABLED
Key Slot 4: DISABLED
Key Slot 5: DISABLED
Key Slot 6: DISABLED
Key Slot 7: DISABLED
[root@gandalf ~]#
```

10. You can delete or revoke keys at any time. We will delete the key from slot 1:

    # cryptsetup luksDelKey /dev/loop0 1

```
[root@gandalf ~]# cryptsetup luksDelKey /dev/loop0 1
Command successful.
[root@gandalf ~]#
```

11. Now you can install Ubuntu into this mounted file system following the steps that we have used earlier in this book. After you complete installing Ubuntu, unmount the filesystem.

12. Add the definition of the encrypted filesystem to /etc/crypttab. The retry parameter specifies the maximum number of times that you will be asked to re-enter password when a wrong or invalid password is provided. The check parameter specifies the type of the file system that is to be mounted:

```
encrypted_feisty /dev/mapper/encrypted_feisty_luks  none  luks,
      check=ext3,retry=5
```

13. Add the device to the file systems that are mounted upon boot in /etc/fstab:

```
/dev/mapper/encrypted_feisty_luks /mnt/feisty_luks ext3
            defaults 0 2
```

14. When you reboot, you will be asked for the passphrase before the file system can be mounted. Provide the passphrase and the file system will be mounted. Now you can start up your Ubuntu guest domain as usual using a domain configuration file.

What Just Happened?

LUKS is an extension to *dm-crypt* and allows us to add multiple users/passwords (up to eight users). LUKS specifies a platform independent standard on-disk format and facilitates interoperability among different software. It uses a partition header to store the encryption-setup information and this enables some of the following options:

- Modifying an encrypted volume's passphrase without any re-encryption of the data present on the volume.
- Provide multiple passphrases for the same data on the volume. This enables multiple users to have access to the volume.
- The ability to transport or migrate data to different systems.

Summary

In this chapter we explored two different mechanisms for encrypting the root file systems used by Xen guest domains:

- **Device mapper encryption** — A mechanism for encrypting block devices using the cryptographic API provided by the Linux kernel.
- **Device mapper encryption using LUKS** — A standard format for encryption that extends dm-crypt.

In the next chapter, we will explore the options available for the migration of live Xen instances and the restoration of saved Xen domains.

8
Migration

In this chapter we will discuss the migration of domains from one server to another. You can use two different techniques to migrate a domain. You can save a copy of the domain and then restore the domain on a different server, or you can migrate a domain while it is running, causing minimal service interruption.

We will use the following ways to migrate a domain:

- Save and restore a domain
- Live migration

Migration Requirements

The following are the setup and network requirements for migration:

- Both the source host and destination host must be running Xen and the xend daemon.
- The destination host must have enough disk space, memory capacity, and resources to run the domain after the migration.
- The source host and destination host machines must have the same architecture and virtualization extensions. For example, if the source host is running on x86-64 architecture with extensions, then you must ensure that the destination host does the same. This is stipulated so that you don't run into any mismatches in the instruction sets used by the kernel and the user libraries.
- The source host and destination host machines must be on the same layer-2 network subnet. When a domain is migrated, the migration will not be completed successfully if the destination node is on a different subnet, as the MAC and IP addresses of the domain are moved with it.

- The process of migration causes the xend daemon to stop the domain running on the source host, copy it over to the destination host, and then restart the domain. The xend daemon accepts migration requests from the localhost by default. To allow the migration target to accept incoming migration requests from a remote host, you must modify the destination host's `xen-relocation-hosts-allow` parameter in the `/etc/xend-config.sxp` file. There is no authentication provided, so for security reasons you must restrict the hosts that are allowed to migrate.
- If you are running a firewall, you may need to create explicit iptables rules to permit incoming migration connections.
- Typical migrations result in a downtime of as little as 60-300ms.
- You will need to reconnect to the console of the domain on the new Xen server after the migration. Your existing console connection will not be carried over along with the migration.

Saving and Restoring a Domain

The current state of a running domain is saved in a file on the disk. Xend restores the state of the domain by using this file. This is similar in concept to the hibernation feature of a laptop. During hibernating, a laptop saves an image of the disk state and shuts itself. To come out of the hibernation, it uses the saved disk image to restore the running state.

In this section we will learn how to save an active domain to a file that can later be used to restore the file to the active state either on the same server or on a different Xen server. You must ensure that you have enough disk space to save the image files before you try to save a domain to an image file.

Time for Action—Migrate Domains on your Xen Server

We will create a Debian domain and save its state to a file that will be used to restore the domain.

1. Create the Debian guest domain:

   ```
   # xm create debian_etch_domU.cfg -c
   ```

2. Check to see that the domain is up and running correctly. Since we provided the `-c` parameter to the `xm` command above, the guest domain will start up in the current console. To check whether the domain has started up, you will have to use a different console session.

```
[root@gandalf ~]# xm list
Name                                      ID   Mem VCPUs      State   Time(s)
Domain-0                                   0   129     1     r-----    138.4
debian_etch_domU                           1    64     1     -b----      2.1
[root@gandalf ~]#
```

3. We will save the current state of the domain to the `/xen-saved-images` directory; you can save to a directory of your choice:

```
# xm save 1 /xen-saved-images/etch.save
```

4. Saving a domain will remove it from the list of domains that are currently running. You can check this by using the `xm` command to print the current domains.

```
[root@gandalf ~]# xm list
Name                                      ID   Mem VCPUs      State   Time(s)
Domain-0                                   0   129     1     r-----    344.2
[root@gandalf ~]#
```

5. Restore the saved domain from the file:

```
# xm restore /xen-saved-images/etch.save
```

6. Run the `xm` command again; we should see the restored domain back in the list of current domains.

```
[root@gandalf ~]# xm list
Name                                      ID   Mem VCPUs      State   Time(s)
Domain-0                                   0   129     1     r-----    489.4
debian_etch_domU                           2    64     1     -b----      0.0
[root@gandalf ~]#
```

What Just Happened?

We took an active running Xen domain and saved its running state to a disk file. Please keep in mind that this file is not encrypted in anyway, so a malicious user who gets access to the directory with the saved image files can tamper with the images. It very important to secure all access to the folder that contains these saved images.

The running state of a domain is a snapshot or image of the domain at the time of saving. All the running process information and state are saved to this file. You can examine the file and you will see that it is a rather large binary file. The size of this file will be equivalent to the memory that was being used by the domain when it was saved. So on a reasonable Xen domain that is running some enterprise applications, the size of this file can be very large—in the order of a few gigabytes. Therefore, you must ensure that you have enough storage space where this file is saved. In this example we saved the state to a disk file but there is no reason why you cannot save this file to a large enough network folder or even mounted USB key. Saving the domain to a USB key is a nifty way for you to carry your domain around in your pocket and restore it on a different server!

A saved domain is restored by using the `restore` option with the `xm` command. This will start up the domain again and restore it to the state the domain was in when it was saved. There are some things you need to keep in mind when using the save and restore feature:

- The ID of the restored domain will be different from the ID the domain had when it was saved. So when you use `xm` to view a restored domain, you will notice that the ID is different.
- The domain is restored to its earlier state (when it was saved) but you will not be automatically connected to the domain's console. You will need to explicitly run the `xm` command to connect to the console.
- This is a simple and easy way to migrate your domains, but please note that as the domain has been removed from the active domains while being saved, the services running on the domain will no longer be available or accessible. If this service interruption is unacceptable to you, you should consider the live migration feature of Xen that we will discuss in the next section.

Live Migration

In the previous section we explored the simplest way to migrate domains on your Xen server. This simple way will not be an option in cases where you have SLA on your servers or where you want to minimize the interruption of services. Xen provides a powerful feature called live migration that lets you migrate running domains to a different Xen server with minimal disruption to the services. In this section we will discuss live migration and the process that Xen goes through under the covers in order to make it happen.

Time for Action—Relocation of an Active Running domain

The server configuration that we will use for live migration consists of the following:

- **palantir**: A Xen host server that will run a Ubuntu Feisty guest domain, which uses a NFS exported directory.
- **boromir**: A Xen host server that serves as the destination for the migration of the Ubuntu Feisty guest domain from the palantir server.

- **frodo**: A linux NFS server that will provide the storage for the Xen domains over the network.

The following diagram shows the configuration.

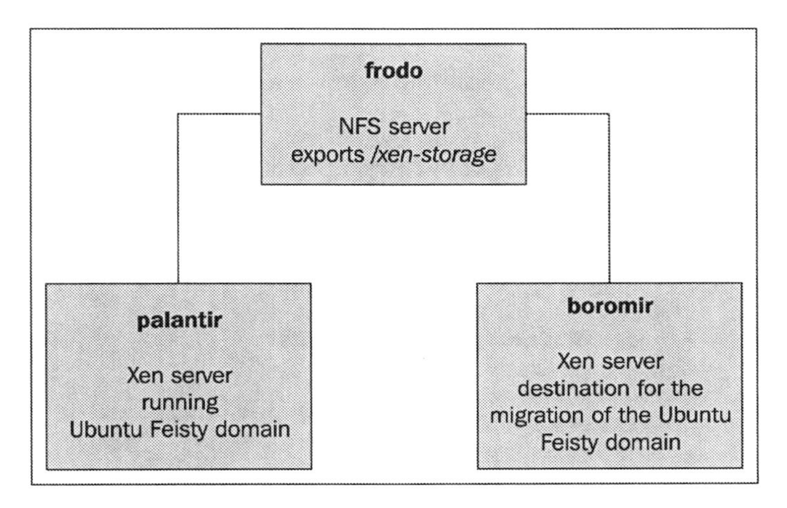

1. Live migration needs shared storage. A practical minimum network requirement would be a 100 MB network. The other setup related requirements for migration are mentioned earlier in the chapter. So let us set up a NFS server on our first Xen host for sharing storage. The domain that we will be migrating will run off the shared storage space on the NFS server. Chapter 6 shows you the steps needed for getting the NFS server installed and working.
2. Edit `/etc/exports` and add the following line to export the storage directory:

```
# /xen-storage *(r,sync,no_root_squash)
```

3. Save the file and restart the NFS server. Add the NFS server to the services on the server and set it up to start on reboot:

```
# service nfs startchkconfig nfs on
```

4. We need to set up the two Xen servers so they can use the NFS server exports for storage. Add mount points on each of the two Xen servers to mount the exported directory:

```
# mount palantir:/xen-storage
# mount boromir:/xen-storage
```

5. Modify the xend configuration file to allow live migration. Edit the `/etc/xen/xend-config.sxp` file and ensure that the following two lines are not commented out:

   ```
   (xend-relocation-port 8002)
   (xend-relocation-address '')
   ```

   This will enable the Xen daemon to listen to and respond to requests for live migration:

6. Follow the steps that we used in Chapter 6 for getting a Xen domain running on a NFS server storage. Start up the guest domain on palantir. Use the following configuration for the guest domain:

   ```
   cat > /home/pchaganti/xen-images/ubuntu_feisty_nfs_domU.cfg <<
             "EOF"
   kernel = "/boot/vmlinuz-2.6.16.38-xenU"
   memory = 256
   name = "ubuntu_feisty_nfs_domU"
   vif = [ 'ip=192.168.1.111' ]
   nfs_server = '192.168.1.67'
   nfs_root    = '/xen-storage'
   root        = '/dev/nfs'
   EOF
   ```

7. Now we have a guest domain running on palantir that is using the NFS exported directory for storage. You can check whether the domains are running correctly by using the `xm` command on palantir.

8. We will live migrate this guest domain to the boromir server. This will take several minutes before completion. If the migration fails to complete successfully, a message indicating the failure on the console will be shown.

   ```
   # xm migrate --live ubuntu_feisty_nfs_domU boromir
   ```

9. That's all it takes to migrate a live running domain to another Xen server! If you use the `xm` command to list the running domains on both palantir and boromir servers, you will see that the migrated domain now only appears on the boromir server and is no longer displayed in the list of running domains on the palantir server.

What Just Happened?

Live migration is the movement of a virtual machine from one physical host to another while continuously powered-up. This process takes place without any noticeable effect by the end user and allows an administrator to take the physical server offline for maintenance or upgrading without subjecting the users that are using the virtual machines to downtime.

We modified the default xend configuration file in order to enable relocation of domains. Keep in mind that you need to reboot the host for the Xen server to make the host accept your changes. We changed the following settings:

- **xend-relocation-server** : This is a flag for enabling/disabling the relocation server. By default, this is set to `no` to keep the relocation server deactivated. During the process of migration, the domain virtual memory is exchanged in raw format without any encryption. Make a note of this before enabling this in an untrusted network.
- **xend-relocation-port** : The port used by the xend daemon for relocation. The default value for this port is 8002.

There are a couple of other parameters that we did not modify, but which you should be aware of in an enterprise deployment environment:

- **xend-relocation-address**: This is a flag for restricting the migration of the domain only to a specific interface. The address specified is the one that listens for connections coming into the relocation socket. This flag will only be used if you also enable the `xend-relocation-server` parameter.
- **xend-relocation-hosts-allow**: This is a flag that defines the hosts that are allowed to communicate with the relocation port. The value is a sequence of regular expressions separated by spaces. If the value is empty, then all incoming connections are allowed. The values can match either an IP address or a fully qualified domain name.

The discussion and diagram in this section of how Xen's live migration feature works is based on the excellent research papers by the Xen team, which are available at `http://www.cl.cam.ac.uk/research/srg/netos/papers/2005-migration-nsdi-pre`. The migration from palantir to boromir can be broken down into a series of steps or interactions between the two Xen servers:

1. **Pre-Migration**: The Feisty domain is running on palantir and is an active domain.
2. **Reservation**: A request for migration is issued to the on palantir, which then checks and confirms that resources are available on boromir. Xend then reserves a VM container of the required size on boromir. If *xend* is unable to get the resources it needs on boromir, then nothing will be done further, and the domain will continue to run as is without any changes on palantir and the relocation effort will be abandoned.
3. **Iterative Pre-Copy**: Memory pages are transferred from palantir to boromir starting with all the pages and only then with the pages that were changed during the initial transfer. Eventually all of the pages will be copied to boromir.
4. **Stop-and-Copy**: The running domain on palantir is suspended and all its network traffic is redirected to boromir. At the end of this stage, there is a suspended copy of the domain on boromir in addition to the one suspended on palantir. The suspended domain on palantir is still the primary copy and in case of any failure at this stage, it will be resumed on palantir.
5. **Commitment:** At this stage if there are no errors or failures, boromir will send an indication to palantir that it has a consistent image of the domain. Palantir will now discard the domain in its Xen server and from this point on, boromir will become the *primary* host for this domain.
6. **Activation**: The migrated domain is activated on boromir. All the device drivers inside the domain are now reattached to the new machine.

The following diagram shows this whole interaction. As you can see there is a lot of stuff happening under the covers to make this operation so smooth and seamless!

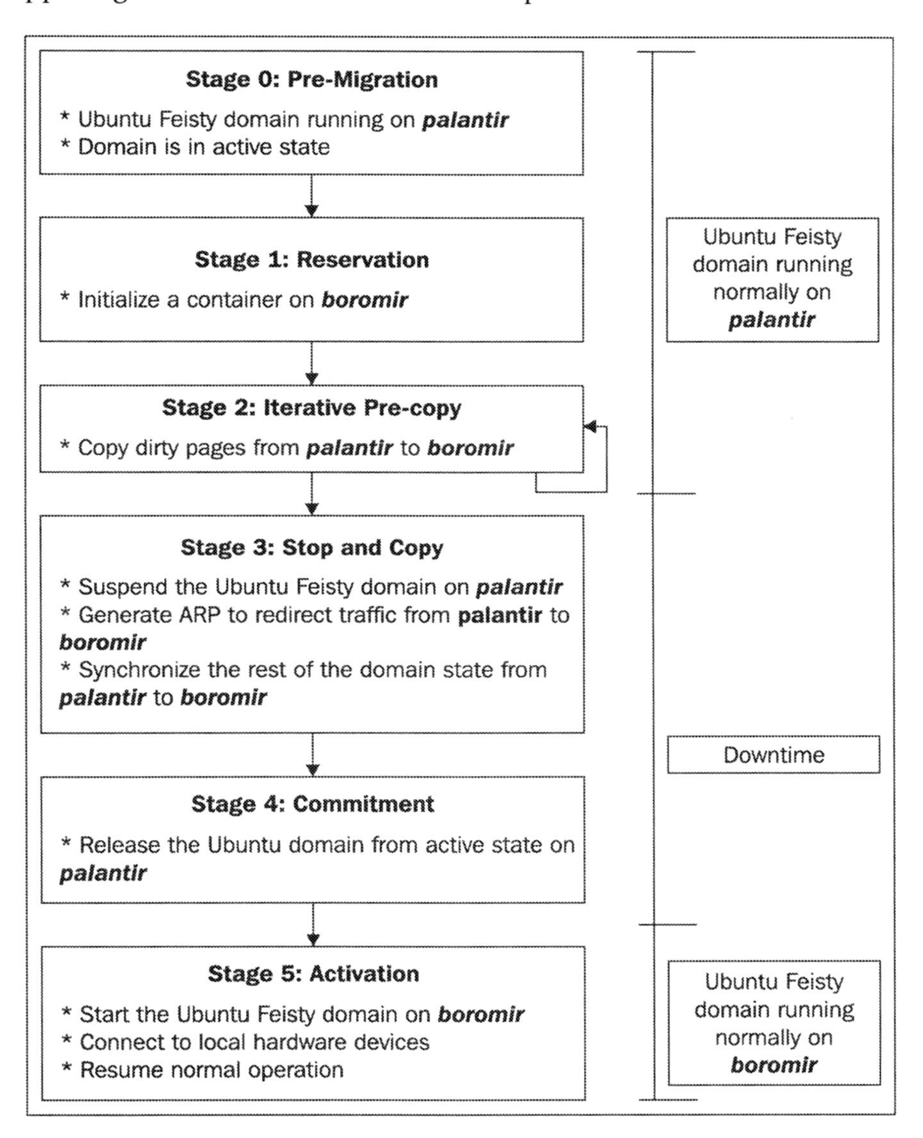

Some of the significant advantages of using Xen live migration are as follows:

- It enables the maintenance of the physical servers that host the virtual machines in a proactive manner. You can monitor the servers and resolve potential and suspected problems by relocating the systems very quickly.
- You can use live migration of Xen along with a high-availability solution such as heartbeat to provide a failover system. The latest versions of Enterprise SuSe Linux Server and Red Hat Enterprise Linux provide high availability solutions using Xen.
- You can meet your Service Level Agreements for services easily and you can avoid any disruption of business critical services.
- It makes the balancing of load across multiple servers possible. This will let you optimize and better utilize the computing resources across the enterprise. There is no support currently in the open source version of xen for automating the migration upon sensing failures in dom0.
- It makes it simple to add more computing power to your system configuration as you need it.
- You can replace hardware as needed without interruption to the services being provided.

Summary

In this chapter we explored two different ways of migrating Xen guest domains:

- **Save and restore**—A mechanism similar to laptop hibernation where the running domain state is captured in an image on the disk and is later used for restoring that domain.
- **Live Migration**—Live relocation of an active running domain with minimal disruption and downtime.

In the next chapter, we will look at some future trends in Xen.

9
Xen Future

In this chapter we will discuss some of the recent enhancements and ideas based on Xen. Most of these are still evolving or are fairly new and will likely change over time. We will discuss the following technologies in this chapter:

- Libvirt
- VMcasting

Libvirt

Libvirt is a virtualization API for interacting with the various virtualization implementations (`http://libvirt.org/index.html`). It is essentially a C API, but provides bindings for a variety of languages, Python being the best supported. It is very actively maintained and supported by the open-source community. In its present form it provides support for accessing Xen virtualization, KVM, and QEMU. However, it is built to be framework independent and provide support for accessing other virtual instances as they become available.

In order to provide the decoupling of the virtualization technology from the API, libvirt defines the following abstract notions of a virtual instance:

- **Node**: A single physical machine.
- **Hypervisor**: Provides the ability to virtualize a node within a set of virtual machines.
- **Domain**: An instance of an OS that runs on a virtual machine. The machine itself is provided by the hypervisor defined above.

Libvirt provides the capability to manage the domains running on a node in a hypervisor instance. To do this in a manner that is independent of the hypervisor technology used, libvirt will need to provide the lowest common denominator of the virtualization support. In this way the API can provide a generic way to manage the domains on the nodes in a hypervisor for any supported virtualization framework. By focusing on the smallest common subset of the operations needed for the management of a virtual domain, libvirt provides the ability and the opportunity to layer new functionality on top of the existing API. This functionality allows it to build applications that can provide a higher level of management tools. This will also enable libvirt to focus on stability in the functions that it provides.

In a Xen environment, user space applications that use libvirt will need to operate in the dom0 environment. These applications can be run in two ways to connect to Xen:

1. Root access:
    - A read/write connection to the Xen store.
    - Use the HTTP RPC layer to connect to xend.
    - Use the hypervisor call mechanism.
2. Normal access:
    - This is mainly used for providing read only functions. The user application will need to connect to a proxy that is running as root and request information.

Libvirt provides the ability to connect to Xen using any of the following languages:

- **C:** This is the main language supported by libvirt.
- **Python**: Bindings are generated from the C API. So they tend to stay up to date longer than other languages.
- **Ocaml**: A recent addition to the list of supported languages.
- **Perl**: A recent addition to the list of supported languages.

We used virt-manager earlier in this book. Virt-manager is a desktop application that displays the currently running domains and their statistics. It uses the libvirt-python bindings (`http://virt-manager.et.redhat.com/`). Xen itself provides an API in its recent versions for accessing Xen virtual instances but it falls short of the capabilities provided by libvirt in many ways:

1. Xen API is not very stable and there is a lot of breakage with every released version of Xen. Things seem to be stabilizing slowly but we are not completely there yet. This can be very frustrating when changing versions of Xen. Libvirt API is much more stable and provides a solid foundation for interacting with Xen as you move or change versions.

2. If you use Xen API, you are restricted to using just the Xen hypervisor. This may be OK in certain cases, but the vendor neutral and vendor independent API provided by libvirt is a lot more attractive and it enables you to keep some of your virtualization options open.

3. Xen API being less stable and still evolving has an API that is fairly difficult to discern and is not very intuitive. Libvirt is easy to use and its design is simple. This is one of the key factors for the adoption of libvirt.

In future, we will see more vendors and application developers using libvirt as the standard API for all of their interaction with any virtualization instances as it provides the most stable and easy to use abstraction currently available.

Vmcasting

Vmcasting is a cool new technology that can automate the deployment of virtual machine images using the popular RSS 2.0 format (`http://www.vmcasting.org/`). The machine image itself is transferred to a client as a `.xvm` archive, which is nothing but a simple tarfile that contains the following items:

- **xvm.xml**: An xml file describing the image archive.
- **manifest.txt**: The contents of the archive along with sha1 sums.
- **mf-signature.asc**: gpg signature for the manifest.txt file.
- **signature.asc**: gpg signature for the xvm.xml file.
- **imagefiles**: Any number of gzip compressed hard disk partition images.

The Vmcasting website provides a download for a Debian image in the above format. The following screenshot shows the contents of the Debian `.xvm` archive.

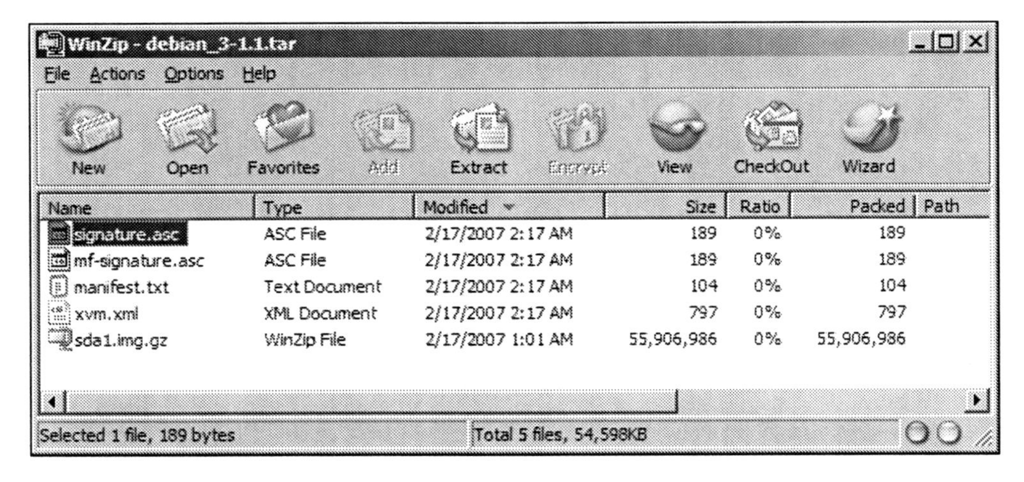

The following is a sample xvm file from the archive:

```
<?xml version="1.0" ?>
<appliance>
  <name xml:lang="en">
    <label>Debian 3.1</label>
    <shortdesc>Debian 3.1</shortdesc>
    <longdesc>
      Debian 3.1 minimal install optimized for XEN
    </longdesc>
    <detail>
      Debian 3.1 minimal install optimized for XEN
    </detail>
  </name>
  <version>1.0</version>
  <vm name="debian 3.1">
    <name xml:lang="en">
      <label>debian 3.1</label>
      <shortdesc>debian 3.1</shortdesc>
      <longdesc>
        debian 3.1
      </longdesc>
      <detail>
        debian 3.1
      </detail>
    </name>
    <memory static_min="128 MiB" />
    <vbd name="sda1" vdi="sda1" mode="RW" />
  </vm>
  <vdi name="sda1" src="file:///sda1.img.gz" variety="system"
              compression='gzip'>
      <name>
        <label>debian 3.1 scsi disk 1</label>
      </name>
  </vdi>
</appliance>
```

This provides a simple and easily readable description of the resources, including the disk partitions, that are available within the archive. The RSS feed containing the above archive as a link looks like the following:

```
<?xml version="1.0" encoding="utf-8"?>
<rss version="2.0">
   <channel>
      <title>Enomalism VMCasting Test Feed</title>
```

```
        <link>http://jamaica/files/test.rss</link>
        <description>Enomalism VMCasting Test Feed</description>
        <language>en-us</language>

        <item>
            <title>Debian 3.1 Base Image</title>
            <link>http://www.vmcasting.org/</link>
            <enclosure url="http://www.vmcasting.org/fileadmin/
               vmimages/debian_3.1.xvm" length="1" type=
                "application/octet-stream"/>
            <description>
                <![CDATA[Debian 3.1 Base Image with minimal components
                  required for growing to a more complete solution.]]>
            </description>
            <pubDate>Fri, 16 Feb 2007 14:43:18 -0800</pubDate>
        </item>
    </channel>
</rss>
```

The `enclosure` tag is a key item that defines an URL attribute that specifies the archive containing the Virtual Machine Image to be downloaded. This is still a fairly new sharing mechanism. It has the potential to provide easy installation and configuration of large blocks of virtual machines at the same time by using a standard definition of a virtual machine. The virtualization management system that you are using will need support; currently only the Enomalism Virtualization Console (`http://www.enomalism.com/`) supports this feature. It will be interesting to see whether it will be supported by any other management applications going forward.

Summary

In this chapter we discussed some of the newer ideas that are gaining ground around Xen.

- **libvirt**: A great API that simplifies access to virtualization instances in a vendor/hypervisor independent way.
- **VMcasting:** A new and innovative way of transferring virtual machine images from the server to the client using the RSS 2.0 format.

Index

G

H

L

M

N

O

P

R

S

U

V

X

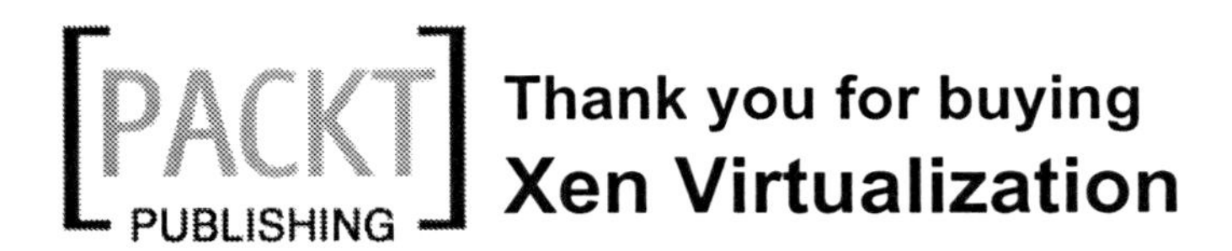

Packt Open Source Project Royalties

When we sell a book written on an Open Source project, we pay a royalty directly to that project. Therefore by purchasing Xen Virtualization, Packt will have given some of the money received to the Xen project.

In the long term, we see ourselves and you—customers and readers of our books—as part of the Open Source ecosystem, providing sustainable revenue for the projects we publish on. Our aim at Packt is to establish publishing royalties as an essential part of the service and support a business model that sustains Open Source.

If you're working with an Open Source project that you would like us to publish on, and subsequently pay royalties to, please get in touch with us.

Writing for Packt

We welcome all inquiries from people who are interested in authoring. Book proposals should be sent to `authors@packtpub.com`. If your book idea is still at an early stage and you would like to discuss it first before writing a formal book proposal, contact us; one of our commissioning editors will get in touch with you.

We're not just looking for published authors; if you have strong technical skills but no writing experience, our experienced editors can help you develop a writing career, or simply get some additional reward for your expertise.

About Packt Publishing

Packt, pronounced 'packed', published its first book "Mastering phpMyAdmin for Effective MySQL Management" in April 2004 and subsequently continued to specialize in publishing highly focused books on specific technologies and solutions.

Our books and publications share the experiences of your fellow IT professionals in adapting and customizing today's systems, applications, and frameworks. Our solution-based books give you the knowledge and power to customize the software and technologies you're using to get the job done. Packt books are more specific and less general than the IT books you have seen in the past. Our unique business model allows us to bring you more focused information, giving you more of what you need to know, and less of what you don't.

Packt is a modern, yet unique publishing company, which focuses on producing quality, cutting-edge books for communities of developers, administrators, and newbies alike. For more information, please visit our website: `www.PacktPub.com`.

Pluggable Authentication Modules

ISBN: 978-1-904811-32-9 Paperback: 124 pages

A comprehensive and practical guide to PAM for Linux: how modules work and how to implement them

1. Understand and configure PAM
2. Develop PAM-aware applications and your own PAMs using the API and C
3. How to authenticate users in Active Directory, mount encrypted home directories, load SSH keys automatically, and restrict web and rsh services

---

Configuring IPCop Firewalls

ISBN: 1-904811-36-1 Paperback: 154 pages

How to setup, configure and manage your Linux firewall, web proxy, DHCP, DNS, time server, and VPN with this powerful Open Source solution

1. Learn how to install, configure, and set up IPCop on your Linux servers
2. Use IPCop as a web proxy, DHCP, DNS, time server, and VPN
3. Advanced add-on management

Please check **www.PacktPub.com** for information on our titles

Printed in the United Kingdom
by Lightning Source UK Ltd.
125674UK00001B/63-82/A

9 781847 192486